A Guide to the Diagnostic Teaching of Arithmetic

Second Edition

Fredricka K. Reisman

University of Georgia

CHARLES E. MERRILL PUBLISHING COMPANY

A Bell & Howell Company

Columbus   Toronto   London   Sydney

Published by
Charles E. Merrill Publishing Company
A Bell & Howell Company
Columbus, Ohio 43216

This book was set in Times Roman.
The Production Editor was Cynthia Donaldson.
The cover was prepared by Will Chenoweth.

Library of Congress Catalog Card Number: 77–86315

International Standard Book Number: 0–675–08397–4

1 2 3 4 5 6 7 8 — 83 82 81 80 79 78

Printed in the United States of America

Foreword

Every concerned teacher knows that some children have difficulty in learning mathematics. What teacher has not searched for some clue to why a particular child was having trouble with a lesson? This book offers no panacea. But it does offer a point of view and a strategy: *diagnostic teaching.*

Teaching that is diagnostic in nature attempts first to identify the level of performance of the child and all the relevant information that contributes to that performance. Then the material to be learned is analyzed into its component parts. Finally an instructional sequence is implemented for the child that blends where the child is cognitively and emotionally with the proper part of the task to be learned.

This book is practical for several reasons. First of all, it is a definitive source on the purposes, nature, and use of diagnostic teaching strategies. It provides an overview of the theoretical background that is at the same time most practical. The theory provides a basis for instructional decisions and action. Second, it provides concise suggestions on tools for diagnostic teaching. This makes the *Guide* a reference that the concerned teacher will want to keep handy and turn to often. Third, it provides explicit guidance on how to develop diagnostic teaching skills. The ultimate practicality of the book is that it can help the teacher do a more effective job of helping students learn mathematics.

It is unfortunate if teachers view *diagnosis* as something to be used only when there is a learning difficulty requiring *remediation.* Clearly, diagnostic teaching strategies can enhance the teacher's effectiveness with all students. The matching of the current level of performance and the material to be learned is certainly sensible for any child.

In this *Guide,* Professor Reisman provides a view of the whole child— emotions as well as cognition. Surely every teacher recognizes there is an affective side to learning, school, and mathematics; but some may not be sure how to develop positive attitudes in students. The *Guide* not only provides a cogent introduction to theories of affective behavior, but shows teachers how to assess it and highlights some concerns to keep in mind during instruction.

Professor Reisman presents diagnostic teaching of arithmetic as an understanding of the child, an understanding of the subject matter, and the blending of the two during instruction. The *Guide* provides many suggestions for implementing diagnostic teaching strategies, and its use will make mathematics teaching more successful and enjoyable.

James W. Wilson
Department of Mathematics
University of Georgia

Author's Preface

This manual is directed to preservice and inservice, general classroom, and special education teachers. The book discusses specific techniques for teaching children arithmetic. It describes problems children have in learning arithmetic and discusses the effect the teacher's relationship with the child has on his or her learning elementary school mathematics. Described are skills involved in performing mathematics and ways of evaluating a student's strengths and weaknesses in mathematics.

The teacher is provided with sample lesson plans, a sequential assessment mathematics inventory, sets of performance objectives that represent the basic relationships of elementary school mathematics curricula, individual and class profile summaries, examples of common errors children make in mathematics, and suggestions for meshing instructional activities with information obtained from various diagnostic procedures that are presented.

Also included are practical applications of Bloom's cognitive taxonomy, Gagne's hierarchy of learning types, Bruner's modes of representing content in mathematics, diagnostic readiness activities based upon Piagetian developmental tasks, and Brownell's discussions of didactic versus guided discovery teaching and levels of learning.

To provide diagnostic techniques for the affective domain—the emotional aspects of learning—use is made of Krathwohl's affective taxonomy, Carl Rogers' concept of an integrated person, Maslow's hierarchy of needs, and Osgood's semantic differential.

The philosophy which underlies this book is that teachers of elementary school mathematics can develop diagnostic teaching strategies. These strategies involve building teacher-made diagnostic tests, developing clinical assessment skills including probing during interviews with students, developing skills in selecting curriculum that is relevant to student needs, and providing appropriate instructional activities.

Acknowledgments

My deep appreciation to William Hays, vice-president for academic affairs, University of Texas at Austin, for his support of the importance of meshing mathematics with psychology. To E. Paul Torrance, chairman of educational psychology, University of George, my gratitude for his continuing encouragement and guidance. To Katherine Blake, acting chairman of special education, University of Georgia, thank you for your recognition and acceptance of the diagnostic teaching system that is the underlying structure of this book. To colleagues at the University of Georgia, especially those in the division of early childhood—middle school education, in mathematics education, and in special education, thank you for your support in helping me refine my thoughts regarding diagnostic teaching of mathematics.

I am grateful to the staff at Charles E. Merrill. My thanks to Fred Kinne, administrative editor, who was extremely helpful throughout production of this text; Cynthia Donaldson, who provided quiet, businesslike service as production editor; Gail Brown, as a member of the sales force, who was professionally supportive; and a final thank you to Steve Branch who, although no longer with Merrill, started it all.

Finally, to my students—you who guide children in learning mathematics—thank you for replacing anxiety and gaps in learning with enjoyment and diagnostic teaching of mathematics.

Fredricka K. Reisman
Athens, Georgia

To my father, my daughter,
and to the memory of
my mother

Contents

Figures

Part 1

What Is Diagnostic Teaching?

1

Introduction to the Diagnostic Teaching of Elementary School Mathematics

Anyone involved in guiding a child to learn a portion of curriculum encounters a two-sided problem. First, the developmental level at which the child is performing cognitively must be identified. Second, the task to be learned must be analyzed in order to determine how many components of the task the child has already acquired. In elementary school mathematics this second phase of the problem, analyzing the mathematical relationships, is the crux of diagnostic teaching. When the teacher is aware of the relationships that are basic to mathematical concepts and generalizations, he or she is better able to make decisions regarding selection of curriculum that is appropriate to the learner and of effective instructional techniques.

For example, in order that a child compute a long division problem, he must be able to multiply and subtract. To multiply, he or she must be able to translate the idea of a certain number of groups, each of a particular size, into a multiplication example (five groups of three = five threes = 5×3). In order to subtract, the child must be able to find the remainder when given a whole and a known part, and if renaming (borrowing) is involved, have a working knowledge of how a place value system operates.

Unless the teacher is able to analyze the relation or task to be learned into its prerequisite parts, he will not know at what level the child's learning has terminated. *The meshing of the steps of the learning hierarchy into the developmental level at which the child is performing is the heart of diagnostic teaching.*

Of course, diagnostic teaching is not only for children having difficulty in arithmetic. All children—whether they are slow learners, average, or

3

very bright—profit from diagnostic teaching because of its basic assumption, the necessity for meshing curriculum with the student's developmental learning level.

New sequences of instruction also may emerge from diagnostic teaching. For example, let us consider teaching the skill of telling time to the precision of a minute. The traditional approach is to teach time on the hour first, then to the half-hour, and next to five minutes after the hour. The child is not guided to tell time to the minute until the last step in the sequence. In fact, many elementary school mathematics texts introduce the fractional idea of "half after" and "a quarter after" the hour prior to the concept of "so many minutes after." However, when looking at how children learn to count, we see that a child learns to count by ones first. Yet, he does not learn to tell time to the minute, which is based on counting by ones, until the latter part of the time-telling sequence, a point which usually is reached during second or third grade. This seems in opposition to the natural mathematical development of counting. Also, it is possible that children become fixated on the positions of time to the hour and to the half hour, thus making it more difficult for them to learn to tell time to the minute. When we analyze the task from a mathematical view and mesh our findings with our knowledge of how a child first learns to count, we discover that our sequence of instruction has been backwards.

Further investigation, making use of Bruner's enactive level of learning, has indicated that children can reproduce time on a clockface before they can identify it. Thus, setting time on a clockface should precede reading time on a clockface. This sequence usually is ignored and, in fact, time-telling instruction often starts at Bruner's iconic or picture level which is exemplified by pictures of clockfaces in arithmetic texts or workbooks (*3*).

Since most young children are used to working with the idea of a number line, instruction can begin with the child's counting from 0 to 60 on a number line. Demonstrated is the concept of one-to-one correspondence as the child matches each number with a minute mark.

I developed a plexiglass clockface for the research on time-telling instruction (*11*) that is based on this notion of reinforcing the "counting by ones" concept. A plastic snap-on simulated a number line from 1 to 60, thus giving the child experiences in counting from 1 to 60. The child then was guided to generalize from this snap-on number line to the sixty minute marks on the clockface. The snap-on number line (from 1 to 60) matched up with the sixty minute marks on the clockface.

The snap-on number line, in addition to having the numerals 0 through 60, also had a number line with 0 to 12 written on it. The numeral 1 on

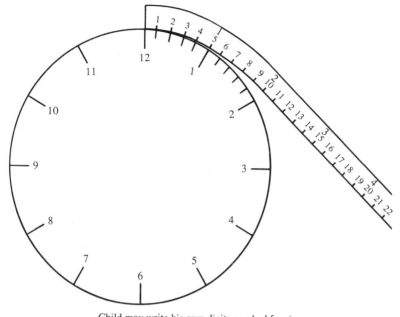

Child may write his own digits on clockface)

Figure 1

Reisman Experimental Clockface

the 12-item number line corresponded to the numeral 5 on the 60-item number line; the numeral 2 (on the 12-item number line) corresponded to the 10 (on the 60-item number line); the numeral 3 corresponded to the numeral 15, etc. The 12-item number line also corresponded to the clockface digits illustrating the underlying multiplication relationships that one group of five is 5, two groups of five are 10, three groups of five are 15 . . . eleven groups of five are 55, and twelve groups of five are 60. Thus, the digit 2 on a clockface means two groups of five minutes after the hour or ten minutes after the hour, while the digit 11 means eleven groups of five or fifty-five minutes after the hour. The children described the digit 12 on the clockface as showing twelve fives or sixty minutes after the hour and said that this was another name for zero minutes after the next hour.

Since the child was actively involved in manipulating the snap-on number line, in naming the minute marks from 1 through 60, and in matching the digits on the clockface with multiples of 5 on the snap-on number line, he was able to analyze a clockface and describe the function of each part.

The minute hand alone was then attached and used as a counter for the snap-on (now circular) 60-item number line. Then the hour hand was attached and used as an indicator of how many times the minute hand had traversed the entire clockface.

Children as young as first graders and a few in kindergarten learned to write the numerals from 1 to 12, properly sequenced, on the plexiglass clockface as they were guided by the snap-on number line.

The language in the initial stages of instruction consisted of "so many minutes after the hour." In my experience in teaching children to tell time, I have found that an early change over to the language "before the hour" is confusing to the child. Piaget, in describing his investigations on learning time concepts, offers an explanation for this "before—after" confusion (9).

Since an analysis of the task or concept to be learned is part of the diagnostic process and since remembering that the child's level of learning and his way of learning also must be investigated, the teacher should become sensitized to looking for new ways to mesh the task at hand with the child's cognitive and affective characteristics.

Diagnosis, then, is a process of determining the facts which need to be taken into account in making academically oriented decisions. Curriculum decisions are dependent upon diagnosing the needs of a particular society, of a unique population within that society, or of an individual child. Decisions about what methods of instruction are most appropriate for teaching a particular topic to a particular type of learner also are determined by diagnosis. Diagnosis involves looking at both the curriculum to be taught and the method of instruction; it may involve asking the following questions: Is the curriculum that I am attempting to teach this child appropriate to his needs, both present and future? Is the concept to be taught appropriate to his mental capacity? Is a learning discrepancy or disability preventing the child from learning? Does the child have the necessary prerequisites in order to learn this curriculum? What is the most appropriate method of instruction that I can use to teach this knowledge to this type of learner? Why has this child not acquired this portion of curriculum, or why is he not able to perform this task?

2

The Diagnostic Teaching Cycle

Diagnosis enables the teacher to determine what content is appropriate and how he or she can help the learner in the best way. The diagnostic teaching of elementary school mathematics involves five processes:

1. *Identifying* the child's strengths and weaknesses in arithmetic;
2. *Hypothesizing* possible reasons for these strengths and weaknesses;
3. *Formulating behavioral objectives* to serve as a structure for the enrichment of strengths or the remediation of weaknesses (see Mager, 1962, and Popham and Baker, 1970);
4. Creating and trying *corrective remedial procedures* (see Glennon, 1963; Glennon et al., 1970; Reisman, 1977; Reisman and Kauffman, in press, for further suggestions);
5. *Ongoing evaluation* of all phases of the diagnostic cycle to see if progress is being made in either getting rid of troubled areas or in enriching strong areas.

This "diagnostic teaching cycle" is pictured below.

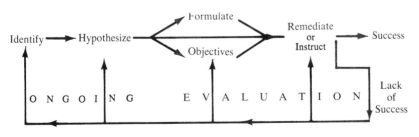

Figure 2

Diagnostic Teaching Cycle

7

The *identification* process involves analyzing such behavior products as achievement test scores, scores on teacher-made tests, responses to mathematical problems during an interview by the teacher, or any other appropriate sample of the student's behavior. The identification component of diagnosis depends upon the teacher's skills in using a diagnostic strategy. These skills involve the ability to construct a diagnostic instrument, to interpret the results of tests and interviews, and to utilize techniques for investigating the child's thinking processes.

Once a student's areas of difficulty in learning mathematics have been identified, the *hypothesizing* function comes into play. What might be the reasons for the particular problems identified? Do the diagnostic results indicate physical, cognitive, or emotional causes, or a combination of these? Do they stem from the student's out-of-school environment, from his school experiences, or from intellectual and emotional concomitants within himself? For the most part, a student's problems are not confined to a single cause. The human being is a complex animal and the causes of his problems usually are complex. The diagnostician in the classroom may have to deal with symptoms for an identification of the cause of a problem which is often elusive. The hypotheses serve as a structure to use in focusing attention on the relationship between the symptoms and the instructional procedures.

For example, I tested a tenth grade boy who was unable to multiply such a simple algebraic expression as $a(b + c)$. The boy scored in the above average range in intelligence, and diagnostic evidence indicated that he was well adjusted emotionally and socially. His work with whole numbers had been successful, and he was able to perform well with abstractions. In algebra, however, he was unable to multiply algebraic expressions. For example, he could not multiply $a(b + c)$ or $(a + b)$ $(c + d)$, and he could not factor $(ab + ac)$. It was hypothesized that the student's difficulty was in the cognitive domain and stemmed from a knowledge gap in his mathematical structure. It appeared that this boy needed to generalize the Distributive Property of Multiplication over Addition [for any three numbers $a, b,$ and $c, a(b + c) = (ab + ac)$] from whole numbers to algebraic expressions. I believed that since the boy was able to identify the Distributive Property with whole numbers in such an example as $7 \times 38 = 7 \times (30 + 8) = (7 \times 30) + (7 \times 8)$, a carry-over of its role in multiplying algebraic expressions would help. I found that he saw no connection between the Distributive Property in the above example with whole numbers and its use in multiplying algebraic expressions such as $a(b + c)$. Further inquiry showed that his algebra instruction had made no use of his whole number knowledge of the Distributive Property. This information led to instruction with more emphasis on meaning and a subsequent demand on his part to understand what he was doing. He was amazed to discover that $a(b + c)$ operated in the same way as 7×38. He was guided to set up a comparison table which allowed him to see the step by step analogy:

	Arithmetic	Algebra
Step 1.	7×38	
Step 2.	$7 \times (30 + 8)$	$a(b + c)$
Step 3.	$(7 \times 30) + (7 \times 8)$	$(a \times b) + (a \times c)$
Step 4.	$(210) + (56)$	$ab + ac$
Step 5.	266	

The renaming of the number 38 as the sum $30 + 8$ was compared to the sum $b + c$ in step 2. The Distributive Property was identified in step 3, and step 4 was said to involve the closure principle for multiplication. To help this boy with the concept of factoring, it was now a simple matter of reversing the above algebraic example as follows:

$$ab + ac$$
$$a(b + c)$$

The principle of identifying a common factor also was compared to whole number situations and the student remarked that it was easier to identify the common factor in algebra since the letters kept their original name.

The comparison of common factors in both the number examples and the algebra examples served as a bridge for the student which allowed him to proceed with algebra by using the Distributive Property of Multiplication over Addition in factoring algebraic expressions. Once he had acquired this structure, he then was able to perform in new situations employing the same axiom. The hypothesis that the boy just mentioned needed guidance in applying the Distributive Property to algebraic expressions was verified by his success in working similar problems.

Guiding a student to see the structure of mathematics is not reserved for gifted mathematics students alone; it can also be an effective remedial strategy. Not only does the mathematics structure become a useful tool for the student from an intellectual or cognitive view, but learning the material also serves to raise the student's self-concept and has a positive effect on his emotional well-being.

The *behavioral objective* which served as the structure for his remediation was: To apply the Distributive Property of Multiplication over Addition to algebraic expressions. Both the content involved and the behavior desired were included in the statement of the objective. The content dealt with the Distributive Property while the desired behavior was application of this content to a new and broader content, algebraic expressions. A behavioral objective, then, includes the concept or task to be learned and specifies what the child is to do that will show that he has acquired a particular concept. Examples of other behavioral objectives and possible techniques of diagnosing whether the learner has attained them follow:

Objective: To complete equations to show the Commutative Property for Addition.
Diagnosis: Complete the following:

$$5 + 3 = 3 + \underline{\qquad}$$
$$\square + \bigcirc = \bigcirc + \underline{\qquad}$$
$$(4 + 5) + (9 + 7) = (9 + 7) + \underline{\qquad}$$
$$(4 + 5) + (9 + 7) = (7 + 9) + \underline{\qquad}$$

Objective: To show the Commutative Property for Addition with dot pictures.
Diagnosis: Complete the picture.

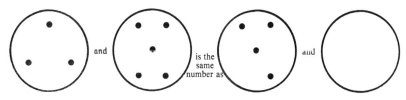

Objective: To state the Commutative Property for Addition.
Diagnosis: Child will state either in writing or orally that the order of two addends will not change their sum.

Objective: To identify the Commutative Property for Addition.
Diagnosis: Draw a circle around the letter for the Commutative Property for Addition.

a. $5 \times 3 = 3 + 5$
b. $5 + 3 = 5 + 3$
c. $5 + 3 = 3 + 5$
d. $(5 + 3) + 2 = 5 + (3 + 2)$

Objective: Underline the step showing the Distributive Property for Multiplication over Addition.

Diagnosis:
$$7 \times 983 = 7 \times (900) + (80) + (3)$$
$$= (7 \times 900) + (7 \times 80) + (7 \times 3)$$
$$= 6300 + 560 + 21$$
$$= 6881$$

Objective: To indicate examples of the Distributive Property for Multiplication over Addition.

Diagnosis: Draw a circle around the letter showing the Distributive Property of Multiplication over Addition.

a. $\square + \triangle = \square$
b. $\square + \triangle = \square \times \triangle$
c. $(\square \times \triangle) + 0 = 0 + (\square \times \triangle)$
d. $\square(\triangle + 0) = (\square \triangle) + (\square \ 0)$
e. $(\square \times \triangle) + 0 = \square \times \triangle$

Objective: To write a number as a product of its prime factors.

Diagnosis: Find the prime factors for the following numbers:

$2 = 2^5$

a. $2\overline{|4}$
   $2\overline{|8}$
   $2\overline{|16}$
   $2\overline{|32}$

b. 14
   $2 \cdot 7$

c. 36
   $4 \cdot 9$
   $2 \cdot 2 \cdot 3 \cdot 3$

d. $111 = 3 \cdot 37$

Since the face value of the digits summed to 3, $1 + 1 + 1 = 3$, 111 was a multiple of 3.

e. 57
   $3 \cdot 19$

Since $5 + 7 = 12$ which is a multiple of 3, 57 is also a multiple of 3. For other divisibility rules see 27th Yearbook, National Council of Teachers of Mathematics (see suggested readings).

The *remediation or instructional* part of the diagnostic teaching cycle depends upon the other components. First, difficulties are identified, then their reasons for existing are hypothesized, and, finally, corrective procedures are undertaken.

Remediation can be either the most frustrating part of the diagnostic teaching model or its most gratifying concomitant. If the remediation yields successful performance on the part of the student who has been experiencing learning difficulties, the rewards are obvious. However, if the remedial procedures appear ineffective, then the diagnostic cycle must be reinitiated and the processes of identification, formation of hypotheses, and formulation of objectives must be brought into operation again. New insights for the diagnostician may arise from the results of the remediation. Perhaps new areas of difficulty that are more closely related to the problem will be identified. These may not have been apparent in the original identification process. New hypotheses may arise that will prove to be more accurate than those already considered. Different behavioral objectives may also emerge from observing the learner's previous behavior.

Remediation which is tutorial in nature is quite different from the concept of remediation described here. Tutorial activities generally start with curriculum that is grade related. For example, a fifth grader having difficulty with addition of fractions with unlike denominators may be tutored at this specific level of mathematics curriculum. However, the remedial activities often need to be directed to lower level tasks such as finding the lowest common multiple (LCM) of two or more numbers; solving indirect open sentences for finding the appropriate name for the multiplicative identity; finding equivalent fractions by using the multiplicative identity; multiplying fractions; understanding relation of denominator to numerator; drilling on basic addition and/or multiplication facts; or possibly understanding the cardinality of sets, since all of these ideas underly adding fractions with unlike denominators.

Take the example $2/3 + 1/5 = $ _____.

Finding the LCM to serve as the new denominator:

3, 6, 9, 12, ⑮

5, 10, ⑮   LCM = 15

Solving indirect open sentences to name the multiplicative identity:

$3 \times \square = 15$ $3 \times \boxed{5} = 15$

$5 \times \square = 15$ $5 \times \boxed{3} = 15$

Finding equivalent fractions by using the multiplicative identity:

$$\frac{2}{3} \times \frac{\boxed{5}}{\boxed{5}} = \frac{}{15}$$

$$\frac{1}{5} \times \frac{\boxed{3}}{\boxed{3}} = \frac{}{15}$$

Multiplying fractions:

$$\frac{2}{3} \times \frac{5}{5} = \frac{10}{15} \qquad\qquad \frac{2 \times 5}{3 \times 5} = \frac{10}{15}$$

$$or$$

$$\frac{1}{5} \times \frac{3}{3} = \frac{3}{15} \qquad\qquad \frac{1 \times 3}{5 \times 3} = \frac{3}{15}$$

Understanding relation of denominator to numerator:

$$\begin{array}{r} \frac{10}{15} \\ + \frac{3}{15} \\ \hline \frac{13}{15} \end{array} \quad and\ not \quad \frac{13}{30}$$

Drilling on basic addition and/or multiplication facts:

$$2 \times 5 = 10 \qquad\qquad 0 + 3 = 3$$
$$3 \times 5 = 15 \qquad\qquad 10 + 3 = 13$$
$$1 \times 3 = 3$$
$$5 \times 3 = 15$$

Understanding cardinality of sets:

All of these sets have 3 elements.

Notice that although the student in the example on page 12 was a fifth grader, he may have to analyze first-grade mathematics if this is where his mathematics weaknesses stem from. Thus, the student's grade in school is irrelevant; it is the level of his knowledge of mathematical relations that determines the nature of the instructional program.

This concept of remediation also differs from the medical model of diagnose—prescribe. The remediation component of the diagnostic teaching cycle presented on page 7 is instructional in nature. The diagnostic teacher must know the mathematics involved in such a way that he or she can determine what mathematics concepts the student needs to know in order to understand the mathematics that is a problem to the learner. The teacher must then be able to translate these prerequisite relationships into learning activities for the student. In addition, such concerns as a child's cognitive style and way of learning are implicit in his program of remediation, but our knowledge in these areas is minimal. Research in how children learn mathematical concepts needs to be coordinated with research dealing with anxiety and learning; knowledge in the areas of personality and perception must be translated into remedial techniques. Finally, evidence concerning the effects of malnutrition, diet, and other medical problems on intellectual development should be investigated to determine their effect on learning.

Instruction may be considered as the verification function of the diagnostic cycle. It is important that the teacher have in mind a strategy for engaging in corrective procedures, and if some improvement is not apparent, he should reexamine his instructional program. If the original identification process led to hypothesizing that a more structured mathematics curriculum was needed, yet, the student's performance became worse when this course was followed, the remediation program might be inappropriate, indeed, might even be harmful. I tested one child in a clinical setting who initially was thought to be in need of indepth mathematics instruction. However, when the results of psychological testing were considered, it was agreed that this child was in a highly anxious state and that a more effective remedial program would involve an easing-off on arithmetic involvement. The child had become the victim of a vicious cycle. His parents demanded high achievement in mathematics and became extremely tense when he did not meet their standards. Eventually, a pattern developed whereby the child became so tense during arithmetic tests, especially timed exams, that he would become physically ill. Thus, in this case, if a more stringent mathematics program had been undertaken, the emotional block to his learning mathematics probably would have worsened. The frightening aspect of this case is that the boy had done such a good job of covering his anxiety that neither his parents nor his teacher had been aware of the extent to which it had developed until the physical symptoms became apparent. The remedial suggestions included placing him in untimed situations when mathematics was involved, lessening demands for high achievement in mathematics, letting him know that he was loved and accepted with no strings (such as buying love with high achievement), and allowing him to team up with a friend in some test situations. The teacher reported that this idea of team test-taking led to a more relaxed test atmosphere for all of the students.

The ongoing nature of the fifth step in the diagnostic teaching cycle, *evaluation,* is very important as a feedback agent. If success emerges from the cycle, the teacher will know that he is on the right track. He evidently has identified the areas of weakness if a child has previously had difficulty with a mathematical task or concept and is now showing growth in this area. By evaluating his hypotheses or reasons for the difficulty, he can check out various possibilities for the lack of learning and is thereby guided through the rest of the diagnostic teaching cycle.

The appropriateness of the behavioral objectives that emerge from components 1 and 2 depends upon the degree of success the child displays in the remediation part of the cycle. If the instructional objectives formed an appropriate remediation program, then the child will display knowledge of the mathematics.

Parts 1, 2, and 3 of the diagnostic teaching cycle (identifying, hypothesizing, and formulating behavioral objectives) are very much dependent upon one another. This triumvirate gives direction to the teaching phase of diagnosing by specifying content and techniques of instruction appropriate for the particular learner.

Evaluation of the program of remediation includes both cognitive and affective aspects. Does the child display the desired learning product and does he perform in an independent, happy, willing manner? The teacher should not be satisfied if only one of these conditions is met. For example, if a child now can solve mathematical sentences but appears hostile, anxious, or fatigued, this should be an indication of the need to formulate some corrective objectives in the affective domain.

Difficulties students encounter when they attempt to solve mathematical problems have been found to come from a number of circumstances. Sometimes the nature of the mathematics problem has been misunderstood. This case might be associated with a weakness in reading ability whereby the student does not comprehend the meaning of the problem. Misinterpreted directions may yield an unacceptable answer from the teacher's point of view, even though the answer would have been acceptable in light of the student's interpretation. For example, the teacher may accept 1/3 but not 2/6 or 12/36 as a correct response. The student may refuse to attempt any solution which appears abstract or complex because he is certain that it will be too difficult for him. This may indicate an inability on the child's part to transfer his knowledge to a new problematic situation. He may not have developed the necessary structure for planning an attack on a particular type of problem; he may lack a necessary prerequisite for the mathematical task because he was absent when a concept was taught, because he has forgotten it, or because he never learned it even though he was physically present. Diagnosis directs attention to such possibilities as well as to instances where children fail on purpose because of some need or emotional block. Emotional blocks are often the reason for bright children doing poorly in elementary school mathematics.

The evaluation process not only provides feedback to the teacher, but the learner also receives immediate reinforcement which guides him to continue along the same route or to change course to accomplish an objective.

**Comparison with
Other Subjects**

When the teacher identifies areas of difficulty in learning mathematics, he or she often compares the student's performance in learning mathematics with his performance in learning other disciplines. This affords a baseline of information for the student's academic achievement in general. If his overall achievement is low, an investigation of his total educational experience is warranted, as is the obtaining of some measures of his mental ability. Is the low achievement in all areas a function of the youngster's out-of-school environment, or is it due to limited ability? Of course, one must realize that measures of ability which show up as being limited need to be scrutinized because they may be a reflection of an inappropriate test.

If the area of low achievement is apparent in mathematics alone, then the causes may be emotional in nature or may possibly stem from ineffective mathematics teaching. I tested several children who were failing arithmetic and doing well in other subjects. One girl in grade 7 admitted that she had a man teacher for the first time and was embarrassed to ask questions when she did not understand something in math class. She was usually a good student and believed that "things would clear up" as they went along. However, things did not clear up; in fact, they became progressively worse until the day she came home with a D grade on her report card. This grade prompted a teacher-parent conference; consequently, the girl was referred to a university-based clinic for diagnosis. The results of the diagnosis were discussed with both the parents and the girl's mathematics teacher who encouraged her to speak up when she needed help. The teacher initiated a diagnostic approach in his teaching and told how he now identified other students with learning difficulties and found that these difficulties were remedied easily once they were diagnosed. He said this case had made him aware for the first time that low performance on class tests may stem from a myriad of reasons and that he would question his students about their answers instead of just recording test results.

Another student also was doing well in all areas except arithmetic. This boy was in third grade and his parents were worried that he would not be admitted to engineering school if his grades in math did not drastically improve. The father was an engineer and wanted the boy to follow in his footsteps. An analysis of the boy's mathematical concepts, computation skills, and verbal problem-solving ability showed that he made many errors in computation, although he had a good grasp of concepts and did fairly well in verbal problem solving. It was ascertained that his grades in arithmetic were based mainly on teacher-made tests that were computational in nature and thus reflected only his weakness in mathematics without showing his conceptualization level. It was suggested to the parents that they ease up on a definite career decision for the boy at this time and that instead of emphasizing his one weak area, they start reinforcing his successes. The teacher also built tests that would sample more than just computation skills and mapped out a plan to help the boy improve his computation performance by using practice exercises and praise for his effort.

3

Why Some Children Have Difficulty Learning Arithmetic

Involved in identifying the areas of difficulty in learning elementary school mathematics are such considerations as the appropriateness of the mathematics curriculum to the intellectual, social, emotional, and psychological needs of the student, and the suitability of past methods of instruction both to the curriculum taught and to the manner in which the student learns. A comparison of his or her performance in learning mathematics with performance in learning other disciplines and an analysis of whether the difficulty lies with learning facts, concepts, or both is helpful. A review of the products of behavior (such as scores on achievement tests and teacher-built evaluations) that were used to identify difficulties with mathematics is important, along with an analysis of the results of performance on appropriate and valid diagnostic instruments.

Possible Causes
of Difficulties

$$2 + 4 = 11$$

If you assume there is no typographical error involved in this addition example and if you have not been exposed to nondecimal numeration systems, then you are probably experiencing some of the same feelings your students have when they are learning to perform addition computations. The problem makes sense, of course, if you identify that the base involved is five and not ten. The "11" means one group of five and one unit which equals six in base ten. However, if the learner does not identify the above statement as a base five addition fact, she will be unable to understand the example's answer.

Problems with mathematics performance may emerge from many sources. Difficulties in learning arithmetic may stem from gaps in the child's mathematical foundation, lack of readiness, emotional problems, deprived environment, poor teaching, or a learning disability.

Gap in Mathematical Foundation

For a child to be able to display skill in arithmetic computation, she must have a basic understanding of the mathematical relationships underlying the computation. If there is a gap in her conceptual foundation in elementary mathematics, she will not be able to perform mathematical tasks which are dependent upon this foundation. For example, division is based upon a knowledge of subtraction, and multiplication.

In looking at the mathematics curriculum, one must consider the level of difficulty involved. If the curriculum contains an abundance of material which is too advanced or too difficult for the student, she may become frustrated and give up. On the other hand, a curriculum that is too easy leads to boredom and the student again may give up. Does the curriculum offer motivation to the student? Can the teacher take advantage of student interest to "hook" the student on learning mathematics or must she follow a school policy that says to "be on page 234 on December 5 or you won't finish the book, and you must finish the book"? In other words, must the book be taught instead of the child?

Is the mathematics implicit in a situation of interest to the child's life? A study by Braun (1969) found that low achievers comprehended "to an appreciable degree" that work with fractions was related to percentages when a homemade radio was used as the visual aid. The children made workable dials using a cycle range for AM of 550–1600 kilocycles and for FM of 80–108 megacycles. The students noted distance in numbers between various stations on a dial beginning with zero, then translated these distances into fractional parts of the dial and, finally, proceeded to rename the fractions into percentages. Braun concluded that the students were dealing with a matter with which they had daily interest because most of them had radios in their homes.

Another concern in looking at the curriculum might be that the student has changed schools and undergone an accompanying change in the mathematics program. With an emphasis on a "back to basics" curriculum, change may result in a new focus on computation using the basic operations of addition, subtraction, multiplication, and division. Relations underlying the various computational algorithms must be understood in order to avoid creating gaps in one's mathematical foundation.

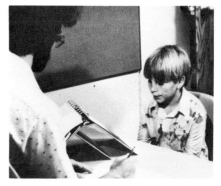

Clinical interviews are used to implement the Diagnostic Teaching Cycle.

The diagnostic teacher considers the child's developmental level, the task, and the instructional strategy.

The curriculum and instruction must mesh with the child's intellectual, social/emotional, and physical needs.

It is impossible for a single published test to tap a total range of mathematics curriculum or provide information for why a child misses one item and has gotten the preceding item correct.

21

Lack of Readiness

Give a five year old a basket of seven apples to count. If she counts in either of the two ways that follow, she has not mastered one-to-one correspondence, which is basic to any work with numbers.

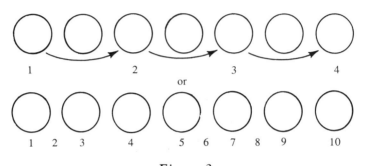

Figure 3

Example of Rote Counting

If she cannot select the larger or smaller of two sets, she lacks a necessary prerequisite for number work. If she cannot label a set with its appropriate number name or numeral, she is not yet ready for computation. The child may not be able to reproduce a set having the same number of objects as a model set. She may not be able to put sets with different numbers of objects in order by going from smallest to largest. She may not recognize that two sets having the same number property (each having the same number of objects) continue to have the same number property even when one set is spread out so that it takes up more space than the other. And she will not understand our place value system of numeration unless she has the concept of many-to-one, the idea that a numeral placed in the tens place means so many tens rather than so many ones. This is a multiplicative idea, yet, the curriculum includes place value in first grade and multiplication principles in third grade.

Emotional Problems

Failure in arithmetic can be caused by emotional problems but it also can cause emotional problems. Some children already have developed a fear of arithmetic before they come to school. They may have heard a parent talk about his difficulty or failure in arithmetic and subconsciously may identify with this parent. A child's previous teacher may have been threatened by the prospect of teaching arithmetic and conveyed these insecurities to the child. Perhaps the child has had a personal experience with mathematics which was negative or unpleasant. She may have been shortchanged at the store and received a severe rebuff from a parent who accused the child of being stupid or of not knowing how to count.

Sometimes, a parent's occupation is mathematically oriented. Such children may have difficulty in arithmetic either because they would rather fail than compete with their parent, or because they try so hard to succeed that they block their learning.

Unfortunately, some parents make their children buy parental love with high grades. Since mathematics is a high-status subject, a child in this position consciously or subconsciously may do poorly or even fail in order to maintain her autonomy. In effect, this child is saying, "Won't you love me for me and not for the high grades?"

I have tested several children having difficulty with mathematics and some with reading problems who seemed to fall into an emotionally based pattern. These children scored in the 115 to 140+ range on the Wechsler Intelligence Scale for Children, yet, they were at least two years below grade level in one or both of these academic areas on standardized achievement tests. The pattern that appeared throughout their case studies also involved the parents of these children. In the majority of cases, the parents were achievement-oriented and were quick to announce that they expected their children to perform at a high level of performance. In those cases where the parents had been informed of the child's I.Q. score by the school or by a psychologist, they were even more upset that their child, with this high ability level, was not working to capacity. The psychologist interpreted the findings in such cases as the child's refusal to buy parental love with high grades. This usually was described as a subconscious act on the child's part because she was unaware of the reasons for her low scores. Similarly, the parents were not aware that this was the demand that they were projecting to the child. I am not certain of the merit of such an interpretation and would rather categorize such an interpretation as a hypothesis, but it is a hypothesis worth pursuing. At any rate, the results of pointing out this possibility to both the child and the parents where treatment involved a psychologist working with the family were successful in some cases. It is interesting that arithmetic and reading, the two high-status school subjects, seemed to be the areas most affected under this hypothesis. Indeed, if the child perceived her parents as demanding that their love be bought with high grades and she was unwilling to do this—either consciously or subconsciously—what better areas than mathematics and reading could there be in which to fail?

The following studies have investigated parental effect on children's achievement in school. Mumpower and Riggs (1970) have hypothesized that there is a positive relationship between a child's achievement in word accuracy and the parental use of pressure on the child for educational achievement. They have suggested that knowledge of this relationship might be helpful to the teacher of reading since it may explain why some children do so well in word accuracy while doing poorly in comprehension. Two groups were matched on age, sex, grade, I.Q., and mental age; any problems that might arise because of differences in race were "controlled by using only white children." One group showed overachievement in word accuracy by one full grade and their comprehension was normal. The other group showed no overachievement in either word accuracy or comprehension. To find factors that might account for the first group's overachievement in word accuracy, a study of the material contained in the subjects' folders was made and ten factors were found. Since the hypothesis was that subjects in Group 1 would show more of these factors than would the subjects in Group 2, it was necessary to test only the significant differences in the factors of Group 1 and Group 2 that were in the yes-no or no-yes cells. The most significant difference between Groups 1 and 2 was that the parents exerted pressure on the children in Group 1 for good grades. These findings suggest that children who overachieved in word accuracy exhibited certain characteristics that children who achieved normally did not exhibit. The overachievers expended much effort in school, evidently in response to pressure exerted on them by their parents. There was a tendency for the overachievers to show signs of emotional disturbance as related to school and for their parents to fail to either understand or accept their limitations. The authors concluded that the children who overachieved in work accuracy were subjected to more pressure than was necessarily good for them. They succeeded by achieving on a lower level of learning which involved rote learning, but failed to do well in comprehension, which required a higher level of mental maturity. The parents of the overachievers needed to understand their children better and to accept their limitations.

Pierce (1961) has suggested that "male underachievers have particularly poor relationships with their fathers." McGillivray (1964) has described the underachiever's home environment as being more punitive. Rouman (1956) found that among 400 children referred to a Los Angeles guidance clinic, academic failure was greatest among those having no adult male in the home. Elementary school-age children were more dependent upon the father's guidance than were younger children. Greatest withdrawal was shown by those having a working mother, and the age of the child was a big factor in determining the child's major problems. Working mothers contributed to 25 percent of the total number of cases in need of psychological help, and girls made up a fourth of the cases sent for guidance. Some children needed help in adjusting to stepparents. Also, home environment problems were strong factors in a child's school problems.

An open and investigative approach is a necessary part of a diagnostic strategy if we are to identify the real problem. It may be that the initial identification is in the area of mathematics, but a comparison of the student's overall performance as well as a history of her performance in mathematics often leads to a further look at parent-child relations or parent-teacher-child interactions.

Since arithmetic is a high-status subject, failures in arithmetic achievement can cause emotional problems. Some of these actually take a physical form, and a child may break out in a cold sweat or become nauseated at the onset of mathematical activities. A few failures in arithmetic can snowball quickly and cause a child to lose confidence in her academic ability in general.

Deprived Environment

Every child is exposed to quantitative experiences in her environment at a very early age. When she recognizes that her friend has more candy, skips rope for a longer time, runs a greater distance in a given time, or gives her the round cookie instead of the square one, the child is dealing with mathematics. However, children who are disadvantaged have meager experiences in number situations. Hilda Taba and Deborah Elkins, in their book *Teaching Strategies for the Culturally Disadvantaged (13),* have described the effects of a deprived environment on learning mathematics concepts:

> Research indicates that the condition of life in slums tends to be meagre in all respects. Slum life provides a minimum range of stimulation and minimum opportunity to manipulate objects or to experiment with them in an orderly manner. Monotony of input limits expressiveness of the output and the ability to perceive precise relationships or other abstract qualities, such as size, shape, distance, and time.*

The teacher, therefore, must provide the following basic quantitative experiences for disadvantaged children: manipulating objects to form sets

---

* Reprinted from *Teaching Strategies for the Culturally Disadvantaged* by Hilda Taba and Deborah Elkins (Chicago: Rand McNally and Co., 1966), p. 7, by permission of the publisher.

of different number; matching objects of one set to objects of another set in a one-to-one correspondence to see if there are any left over in one of the sets; guiding the child to abstract concepts of size, shape, or number from sets of objects; moving from manipulation of objects to activities with pictures of the objects; and, finally, guiding the child to work with symbols, the numerals which stand for the number of objects in a set.

Poor Teaching

Unfortunately, all of the reasons for children's learning difficulties in mathematics do not reside in either the child or society. Some have their origin in the school setting itself, more specifically, in the weaknesses of the teacher.

Concrete manipulatory experiences must be provided in sufficient amounts for each child to build a foundation of such basic mathematical relationships as one-to-one and many-to-one correspondence; more than and less than; combining sets as a model for addition; separating sets as a model for subtraction; and naming the number property, the "how muchness" of a set with word names (five) and with numerals (5). Unless opportunities for learning these basic relationships have been provided, the teacher has been delinquent.

Sometimes the teacher creates an atmosphere in the mathematics classroom that does not encourage asking questions when an idea is not understood. Often, a child will assume that a hazy idea will clear up as time goes on, but finds instead that a gap in her foundation has emerged. Teachers must diagnose constantly to pick up these gaps. Informal paper-pencil quizzes where grades are not recorded and talking with the child can help to identify the child's trouble without seeming to threaten her. An analysis as to whether the child is experiencing difficulty in mathematics as a result of a weak conceptual structure or because of a lack of consolidation of facts necessary to build the particular concepts is essential to remediation. As Brownell has explained, facts are arbitrary associations and contain a minimum amount of meaning (2). They are learned in a rather rote manner, and thus, are in need of practice exercises until they can be handled with facility. Concepts, however, are a different matter. The learning of concepts depends upon conditions associated with the learner, the nature of the task, and the abstracting process.

Learning Disabilities

Inefficient searching strategies, inability to retrieve labels, inability to produce written responses, poor short-term and/or long-term memory, poor spatial relations, impaired communication, and excessive fatigability are symptoms of learning disabilities. Suggestions for diagnostic teaching of mathematics to children having one or more of these discrepancies are included in *Teaching Mathematics to Children with Special Educational Needs* (Reisman and Kauffman, in press).

4

What You Need to Know about Diagnostic Teaching

It is important to realize that diagnostic teaching is appropriate for all children: the gifted, the average, the slow learner, children who excel in mathematics, children who sometimes have difficulty with mathematics, and children who always are troubled by endeavors in mathematics. The diagnostic strategy enables you to create new teaching sequences which are more effective with some children as well as allowing you to identify strong and weak areas in mathematics for one child or the whole class.

In order to visualize effects of a gap in the child's mathematics foundation, think of a weak or broken rung on a ladder. Such a rung can either prevent you from climbing any further, or if you skip over the broken rung, can make you feel uneasy because you know it's there. The rungs on a ladder are the necessary prerequisites for reaching the top.

Analyzing a Skill to Be Learned

For a child to perform a simple operation on numbers, he must have the necessary prerequisites needed to reach the top of his ladder. For example, in order to understand the algorithm $\frac{23}{-9}$, the child must know these prerequisites:

—that 23 means two tens and three ones;
—that 9 means nine ones;

29

—that two tens and three ones may be renamed as one ten and thirteen ones;

—that by renaming two tens and three ones as one ten and thirteen ones, we change only the name but not the number;

—that we obtain this new name by using place value: for every group of ten ones, we must rename them as one ten in order to record the number, since after nine ones, we have no single digit to record ten ones; so we exchange ten ones for one ten, thus moving over to the tens place. In subtraction, when more ones are needed, we merely undo this action, and change one of the tens back to ten ones. These ten ones are added to the ones already there;

—that since the number to be subtracted may not exceed nine ones (or it would have already been renamed as one ten and so many ones), it is sufficient to rename only one of the tens as ten ones, to be added to the number of ones already present;

—that 13 minus 9 are 4;

—that one ten minus zero tens is one ten;

—that "—" means "subtract";

—that the top numeral in a subtraction example stands for the whole;

—that the bottom one stands for the known part that is to be subtracted to find the unknown part:

$$\begin{array}{|l|}
\hline
\text{Whole} \\
\text{—Known Part} \\
\hline
\text{Unknown Part} \\
\hline
\end{array}$$

If any one of these concepts is unknown to the child, he may have difficulty with this subtraction algorithm. This is why you will see $\begin{smallmatrix} 23 \\ -9 \\ \hline 26 \end{smallmatrix}$. The child is making the problem fit what he can handle. He does not know how to get enough ones to subtract nine ones, so he breaks a ground rule and subtracts some of the whole from the part.

It would be wise to provide the child with experiences in place value first, then to diagnose if his weakness is here. He may be able to regroup ten tongue depressors as one bundle of ten at the concrete manipulative level, but he may not see a connection to recording numbers as:

$$\begin{matrix} 1 \\ 2 \end{matrix}$$

$$
\begin{array}{c}
3 \\
\cdot \\
\cdot \\
\cdot \\
7 \\
8 \\
9 \\
10 \\
11 \\
12 \\
\cdot \\
\cdot \\
\cdot \\
19 \\
20
\end{array}
$$

A place value chart will help.

tens	ones	
	1	
	2	
	·	
	·	
	·	
	8	
	9	Renaming occurs here
1	0	
1	1	
1	2	
·	·	
1	9	
2	0	

You must determine if his gap is at the symbolic level or at the concrete level. Since the pictorial level lies between the concrete and symbolic levels of representing numbers, you might guide the child to portray the example $-\underset{9}{\overset{23}{}}$ as shown on page 32.

The teacher must know what prerequisite concepts are necessary for subtracting a number represented by one digit from a number represented by two digits when renaming is necessary. Then, you find out what the student knows and what he or she does not know. Appropriate ma-

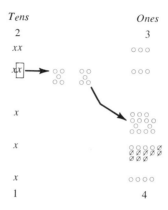

terials and methods are then selected, and you can proceed to fill in gaps in the child's mathematical foundations.

This is diagnostic teaching. You have identified an area of weakness, subtracting with renaming. You hypothesize possible causes for the child's lacking this computation skill, considering, perhaps, an omission of one or more of the prerequisites. You determine what he should be taught and how to teach the missing links. You then give the child similar problems $(32 - 8, 34 - 6, 73 - 9)$ to evaluate whether you need to do more teaching here or whether you can go on because the child has demonstrated that he can now perform this skill.

In the above analysis of the subtraction example $\frac{23}{-9}$, use was made of Gagné's concept of learning hierarchies (4), and of three levels representing curriculum—the concrete level, the pictorial level, and the symbolic level involving numerals (3). These tools are helpful in identifying the sources of weakness in mathematics.

Diagnostic teaching also allows the creation of new sequences of instruction. By analyzing a concept or skill to be taught, the teacher is in a position to set aside traditional teaching sequences and try new approaches. One example of this follows in regard to a time-telling sequence of instruction developed as a result of analyzing the task of telling time to the minute (10). Not only did it become apparent that identifying time on a clockface was a skill rather than a time concept, but it also became clear that children could perform this skill before they had acquired the "measurement of time" concept. In fact, I found that some first graders could reproduce and identify time to the minute on a clockface, although it was not until third grade that children were responding correctly to the Piagetian "measurement of time" tasks (9).

Once you analyze a concept or skill into its parts and rearrange these in a sequence of instruction you may enter the resulting instructional program according to the particular needs of the child. Following is a suggested instructional sequence for teaching the skill of identifying time on a clockface.

Time-Telling
Objectives

1. To say the names of the numerals from 1 to 12.
2. To identify the numerals 1 to 12.
3. To count to sixty by ones using a number line.
4. To recognize that the sixty numerals on a number line match up in a one-to-one correspondence with the sixty minute marks on a clockface.
5. To recognize that the circumference of a clockface is like a number line that is curved.
6. To recognize that the longer minute hand is the pointer for the "60" number line.
7. To count clockwise by ones every minute mark from the zero mark on a clockface to determine the number of minutes after an hour indicated by the longer pointer.
8. To say " _____ minutes after" the hour.
9. To place the numerals 1 to 12 in order on a number line and then count them aloud.
10. To move the numerals 1 to 12 from their number line position to their clockface position.
11. To read aloud all of the numerals on a clockface in a clockwise direction starting at 12.
12. To recognize relationship between the placement of numerals on the "12" number line and the multiples of five on the "60" number line when both number lines are of the same length.
13. To map the multiples of five on the "60" number line onto the "12" number line in a counting sequence using the idea of many-to-one relation.
14. To keep a tally on the "12" number line the number of times one counts to sixty on the "60" number line.
15. To recognize that the tally counter on the "12" number line is doing the same job as the hour hand on the clockface.

16. To show zero minutes after the hour with the minute pointer.
17. To say "o'clock" when the minute hand is at the top center position pointing to the "12" on the clockface.
18. To read _____ :00 as o'clock.
19. To recognize that the minute hand (longer pointer) points to the top center of the clockface when the clock reads _____ :00.
20. To associate the word "o'clock" with " _____ :00" and the top center position of the minute hand.
21. To associate hours with the numeral indicated by the shorter hour hand on the clockface.
22. To determine the hour as indicated by the numeral that the hour hand is pointing to when the minute hand is pointing to the top center of the clockface.
23. To recognize that the longer hand is always pointing to the numeral 12 when the hour hand points directly to a numeral on the clockface.
24. To show a designated time on the clockface; time designated will be time on the hour.
25. To read aloud the time as indicated by the positions of the hands for time on the hour.
26. To say "o'clock" when reading or referring to time on the hour.
27. To identify time on the hour.
28. To recognize that the hour hand moves slowly from one numeral to the next in relation to the movement of the minute hand.
29. To tell time correctly to the minute using the language "after the hour."
30. To recognize that thirty minutes after the hour is the same as (is another name for) "half after the hour."
31. To say "half after the hour."
32. To show time on the half hour.
33. To identify time on the half hour.
34. To say the minutes and hours in sequence, "thirty-one minutes after 7."
35. To count by fives on the "60" number line.
36. To count by fives on a clockface using the numerals one to twelve on the clockface as a guide.
37. To count multiples of five on a clockface as indicated by the numeral on the clockface to which the longer hand is pointing.
38. To say the minutes and hours in sequence when the minutes are multiples of five, "twenty minutes after 4" or "forty-five minutes after 11."
39. To tell time to the minute using the language after the hour with

facility by counting first by fives and then by ones until the position of the minute hand is reached.

40. To recognize that fifteen minutes after the hour is another name for a quarter after the hour, and that thirty minutes after is another name for half after the hour.

41. To say "a quarter after the hour."

42. To recognize that forty-five minutes after the hour is another name for three-quarters after the hour.

43. To recognize that three-quarters after the hour is another name for a quarter before the next hour.

44. To recognize that another name for a quarter before the next hour is fifteen minutes before the next hour.

45. To recognize that forty-five minutes after one hour is another name for fifteen minutes before the next hour.

46. To use the language "after the hour" when referring to the number of minutes the minute hand has traveled past the numeral 12 on a clockface, and use the language "before the hour" when referring to the number of minutes the minute hand must travel to reach the numeral 12 again during a span of sixty minutes.

47. To count in a clockwise direction the number of minutes the minute hand must traverse to reach the numeral 12.

48. To count in a counterclockwise direction from the numeral 12 to determine how many minutes the minute hand must travel before it will reach the numeral 12.

49. To tell time to the minute using the langauge "n minutes after the hour," "n minutes before the hour," "¼ after," "½ after," and "¼ before."

50. To show the correct time on a clockface in response to the language "n minutes after, n minutes before, ¼ after, ½ after, ¼ before," when these times are spoken.

51. To show the correct time on a clockface in response to the written forms: "8:00, 8:16, a quarter after 8, a quarter to nine, 8:30, half after 8, 8:45, 8:53."

52. To draw the hands on a clockface to show designated times.

53. To show time on a clockface expressed in writing.

54. To identify the time shown on a clockface by selecting the correct written response from a set of pictures of clocks.

Another example of a change in the usual sequence of instruction occurs in the teaching of multiplication of fractions prior to the teaching of addition of fractions. For years, children were expected to add fractions with unlike denominators before they had instruction in those concepts prerequisite to the task at hand. However, upon analyzing the concepts involved, it is apparent that the child who cannot rename 2/3 as 4/6 will not be able to add $2/3 + 1/2$. The child must be able to find common denominators and rename equivalent fractions in order to add fractions with unlike denominators.

When you, the teacher, analyze a mathematical task into its parts and reflect on some of your students' errors in performing the particular task, you are gathering information that will help you to mesh the sequence of these parts with the child's rate of cognitive development and with the child's optimal way of learning in terms of concrete, picture, or symbolic representation of concepts and/or relationships involved.

Part 2

Some Tools for Diagnostic Teaching of Mathematics

5

Some Tools for Diagnosis in Mathematics

The following is a list of published tests that may be used for assessment in arithmetic. Care must be taken to inquire of the publisher about the population for which the test was designed to insure its appropriateness to your students. The mathematics content of the test should be examined to insure that it is testing the particular mathematics curriculum of the children involved.

Published Assessment Tests

1. *Noonan-Spradley Diagnostic Program of Computational Skills.* P. O. Box 78, Galien, Michigan 49113: Allied Education Council Distribution Center, 1970.
2. *Stanford Diagnostic Arithmetic Tests.* New York: Harcourt, Brace, and World, Inc., 1966. Level 1 is intended for Grade 2 to Grade 4, while Level 2 is for Grade 4 through Grade 8.
3. *Stanford Early School Achievement Test.* New York: Harcourt, Brace, Jovanovich, Inc., 1969. (Level 1 is intended for Kindergarten and beginning Grade 1.)
4. *A Test of Understandings of Selected Properties of a Number System: Primary Form.* Bloomington: Indiana University Bureau of Educational Studies and Testing, Bulletin of the School of Education, 1966. (For children in Grades 1 and 2.)
5. Ronald C. Welch and Charles W. Edwards. *A Test of Arithmetic Principles, Elementary Form.* Bloomington: Indiana University

Bureau of Educational Studies and Testing, Bulletin of the School of Education, 1965. (For children eight-years-old and older.)

6. Austin J. Connolly, William Nachtman, and E. Milo Pritchett. *Key Math Diagnostic Arithmetic Test.* American Guidance Service, Inc., 1971.

7. Lola J. May and Vernon Hood. *BASE (Basic Arithmetic Skill Evaluation).* Media Research Associates, 1735 23rd Street S.E., Salem, Oregon 97302, 1973.

8. *Fountain Valley Teacher Support System in Mathematics.* Richard L. Zweig Associates, Inc., 20800 Beach Boulevard, Huntington Beach, California 92648, 1972.

How to Use a Standardized Mathematics Assessment

According to the model of diagnostic teaching presented here, none of the above tests are considered diagnostic in nature but rather, they are achievement or survey tests. In fact, it is improbable that a published diagnostic test exists. When considering a classroom of children, it must be assumed that for various reasons, each is performing at a different level of mathematical thinking. Consider two members of a class who miss the same item for different reasons. These underlying causes hold the key for instruction, and this kind of information is not apparent from the test results. It is impossible to construct a test that taps a total range of mathematics curriculum and provides information for why a child misses one item and has gotten the preceding item correct. An analysis of published tests that purport to be diagnostic shows that between most items, several missing concepts may exist. Furthermore, they do not provide enough information as to *why* a child has answered an item or group of items incorrectly. Is the mode (not to be confused with modality) of response preventing the child from correctly answering an item, or is the difficulty due to lack of a mathematics concept or skill? Attention must be given the type of expressive behavior that is called for, as well as to the nature of the curriculum to be learned. Therefore, the teacher must further analyze and interpret the child's performance on these published tests.

Testing for a student's knowledge of concepts that come between items on these grosser measures is by no means a simple task. However, it must be done, and by the regular classroom teacher whenever possible, to insure an effective instructional program in mathematics. This means that the teacher of elementary school mathematics needs to know the mathematics content of at least eighth grade level. In this regard, many college students have been upset with their lack of mathematics knowledge. My suggestion to students expressing such concerns is that they select one area, probably the topic most pressing for their immediate arithmetic teaching needs, and study this indepth for a year. Repeat the procedure using a different topic each year, and at the end of five years, the individual will have learned five topics that he or she must teach. This strategy is more productive than simply being angry at oneself about a lack of mathematics knowledge.

A diagnostic teacher must be able to analyze the mathematics curriculum in order to develop instructional sequences that will fill gaps in a student's mathematical foundation. Protocals must be developed for identifying strengths and weaknesses of a student or group of students that include concrete and picture tasks as well as paper-pencil tests. The results of such assessment may be used as a guide to diagnostic testing in the form of "teacher-made diagnostic tests" that are designed to tap those gaps which are inherent in published tests.

Diagnostic testing and teaching may be used as a strategy for organizing the classroom into instructional groups. The published assessment tests are a helpful first step in accomplishing flexible grouping techniques. For example, after a standardized mathematics survey has been administered, list the members of your class and record the grade score for those students who have scored below grade level. The grade score for each raw score can be found in the test manual which accompanies the published test.

The grade score (or grade equivalent) refers to the average performance of a group of pupils at a particular grade level. A grade score of 58 (or grade equivalent of 5.8) refers to the average achievement of pupils in the eighth month of the fifth grade. By looking up the grade score which corresponds to a specific raw score (the actual score that a pupil makes on the test), you can tell if the student is above, below, or at his actual grade placement.

For example, if the test is administered to a sixth-grade class in October, this would be an actual grade placement of 6.2 (they are in the sixth year of school, and October is the second month of the school year). If a student's raw score is converted to a grade score by means of the conversion tables found in the test manuals for standardized tests and is found to be 6.0, the student's achievement is slightly below that of the typical student in grade 6.2 (see section on *How to Identify the Underachiever,* pages 49–54).

A weak area is determined by converting the student's raw score on the test to a grade score. Those areas that show grade scores one year or more below the actual grade level should be investigated. This type of class survey summary may be used to identify areas in which the entire class is weak, as well as to identify those students weak in a specific area.

A suggested form for a survey summary for a fifth grade, sixth month (5.6) class follows (see page 142 for alternate format):

Class Survey Summary

Date of Testing _____ Test Administered _____

Name	Arithmetic Computation	Arithmetic Concepts	Arithmetic Application
Allen, Mary			
Brown, John			3.8
Crown, Joe			
McCarthy, Helen		4.3	
Michaels, Jon			4.4
Olive, Carol			4.5
Peters, Sue			3.7
Roberts, Sam	4.6		
Rollins, Jack			4.4
Sullivan, Tom		4.6	
Tompson, Jan		4.4	3.9
Victor, Marie			4.5
Williams, Joe			
Wilson, Sue			
Young, Tony	4.4	4.6	3.9
Zellin, Marge			
Zen, Chien			
Zepher, Keith			

A glance at the chart quickly shows that 44 percent of the class had grade scores of at least one grade level below their present grade placement in Arithmetic Application, which includes verbal problem solving. If the rest of the class scored around grade level or only a little higher on this part, there would be strong evidence that the teaching of verbal problem solving in this particular class needs more emphasis.

Those four students showing a weakness in Arithmetic Concepts can be identified easily, as can the two students needing help in computation.

The next step after analyzing the results of a standardized mathematics test is to sample content in the troubled areas indepth. At this point you may want to build your own informal assessments that are tailored to sample concepts which occur between items on the standardized published test.

6

Teacher-Made Diagnostic Tests

Teacher-made diagnostic tests may take the form of checklists, paper-pencil tests, interviews, or observation of children engaged in activities at the concrete, picture, and symbolic levels. For example, in the time-telling instructional sequence, a simple *checklist* of the fifty-four objectives can quickly reflect which steps the student is able to perform. A *paper-pencil* test may include a series of clockfaces whose times are to be indicated. You might *ask* the child to reproduce time on a clockface and tell her to "think aloud," or you may simply observe the child's behavior as she sets a *real clockface*. Teacher-made diagnostic tests not only allow for a variety of response modes, but they also tap the mathematics in narrower bands than published tests. This narrower band, however, is amenable to analyses, and therefore, gaps are avoided that are inherent in standardized published assessments.

The diagnosis for *addition of fractions with unlike denominators* might include the following test items. For the example $1/3 + 1/2$, a teacher-made diagnostic test may be comprised of tasks at the concrete and picture levels, as well as the following items in the paper-pencil mode:

1. Finding the lowest common multiple (LCM) of the denominators 2 and 3;

	1	2	3	4	5	6	7	8	9			
2	2	4	6	8	10	12						
3	3	6	9	12	15							

2. Solving open sentences;

$$3 \times \square = 6, \qquad 2 \times \square = 6$$

3. Renaming the multiplicative identity;

$$1 = \frac{1}{1} = \frac{3}{3} = \frac{2}{2}$$

4. Recognizing that the following notations are equivalent;

$$\frac{1}{3} \times \frac{2}{2} = \frac{1 \times 2}{3 \times 2}$$

5. Using multiplication of fraction algorithm;

$$\frac{1}{3} \times \frac{2}{2} = \frac{1 \times 2}{3 \times 2} = \frac{2}{6}$$

$$\frac{1}{2} \times \frac{3}{3} = \frac{1 \times 3}{2 \times 3} = \frac{3}{6}$$

$$\frac{2}{3} \times \frac{2}{2} = \frac{2 \times 2}{3 \times 2} = \frac{4}{6}$$

6. Using the addition of fractions concept when the denominators are the same number;

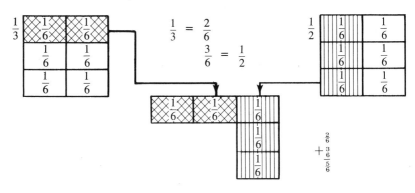

7. Moving from the picture level in task 6 above to using the numerals and algorithms (symbolic level);

a. $\dfrac{1}{3} \times \dfrac{}{\boxed{}} = \dfrac{}{\text{LCM}}$

   $+\dfrac{1}{2} \times \dfrac{}{\triangle} = \dfrac{}{\text{LCM}}$

b. $\dfrac{1}{3} \times \dfrac{\boxed{}}{\boxed{}} = \dfrac{}{6}$

   $+\dfrac{1}{2} \times \dfrac{\triangle}{\triangle} = \dfrac{}{6}$

c. $\dfrac{1}{3} \times \dfrac{\Box}{\boxed{2}} = \dfrac{}{6}$

$+\dfrac{1}{2} \times \dfrac{\triangle}{\boxed{3}} = \dfrac{}{6}$

d. $\dfrac{1 \times \boxed{2}}{3 \times \boxed{2}} = \dfrac{}{6}$

$+\dfrac{1 \times \boxed{3}}{2 \times \boxed{3}} = \dfrac{}{6}$

e. $\dfrac{1 \times 2}{3 \times 2} = \dfrac{2}{6}$

$+\dfrac{1 \times 3}{2 \times 3} = \dfrac{3}{6}$

f. $\dfrac{2}{6}$

$+\dfrac{3}{6}$

$\dfrac{5}{6}$

8. Transferring to addition of fractions with numerators greater than 1.

$$\frac{2}{3} = \frac{2 \times 2}{3 \times 2} = \frac{4}{6}$$

$$\frac{3}{2} = \frac{3 \times 3}{2 \times 3} = \frac{9}{6}$$

$$\frac{13}{6} = \frac{6}{6} + \frac{6}{6} + \frac{1}{6} = 2\frac{1}{6}$$

It is sometimes less threatening to the student if you put the test items on separate index cards. Then you can control the level of difficulty by presenting an easier task if the student seems anxious. It is important to remember that for those children who are overwhelmed by a page of mathematical tasks, one problem on a card may be less threatening. The experience of analyzing a concept into its mathematical components will organize your own thinking and enhance your teaching skills.

7

How to Identify the Underachiever— or Interpreting Grade Equivalents

Very seldom is it enough to look at a child's grade equivalent score on a standardized achievement test to decide whether or not he or she is an underachiever. Since all children do not have the same intellectual capacity, a grade placement score may mean one thing for one child and something entirely different for another. For this reason, it is helpful to be able to determine the child's expected grade equivalent (XGE) based on his intellectual capacity.

Let us assume that a nine-year-old (actually nine years and eight months) child is in the third month of grade four (4.3), has an IQ of 140, and has a mathematics achievement test score of 7.0. The fact that he is in 4.3 grade and has obtained a grade placement score of 7.0 appears to be outstanding. However, in computing his *expected* grade equivalent score, we find this to be 7.4. Thus, he is achieving at a level that is to be expected when considering his high IQ.

Now let us consider another child, also in grade 4.3 and also aged 9.8. However, this child's IQ is 76 and his score on the same mathematics achievement test was 3.1. It appears that this student is not achieving to his fullest. But, when you account for his performance on the test of intellectual ability, you find that he is achieving pretty much at the level to be expected since his XGE is approximately 3.3. For a child to be considered an underachiever, a rule of thumb interpretation is that his grade equivalent scores on normed tests should be ten or more months below his expected grade equivalent score obtained from his performance on tests of mental power that are appropriate to the child's culture and presented in his most facile language. In our hypothetical case, this was not true.

Here are the steps for finding the XGE score:

1. Find the child's IQ. Tests such as the Slosson (12) or the Peabody Picture Vocabulary Test (16) do not require special training as do the WISC (17) or Binet (18).
2. Identify the child's present age and grade in school.
3. Find the child's expected grade equivalent by entering the *Expectancy Scores Table* which follows in the IQ column. Then move horizontally until you come to the most appropriate age/grade column for the child. Read the XGE from the table, or perform the necessary computations within the table as shown in the examples that follow (see table on pages 51–53).

The *Expectancy Scores Table* presents estimates of expected grade equivalents. For example, the approximate XGE for a child who is 8.5 years old with an IQ of 93 is 3.2. This may be found by subtracting the XGE for age eight (2.8) from the XGE for age nine (3.6), finding half of this difference (.4), and adding this to the age eight score ($2.8 + .4 = 3.2$).

Take the example of a child of 11 years and 3 months (11.3). Since the table includes only scores for even ages, some computation will be necessary to find XGEs for years and months. Following is a step by step procedure for finding XGE for ages other than +.5 of a year as was shown in the above example.

Child's Age	IQ	Range of Child's Age	Range of Child's XGE	Child's XGE*
11.3	119	11.0–12.0	7.4–8.8	7.8

* a. Find difference of range of child's XGE in table ($8.8 - 7.4 = 1.4$).
  b. Multiply this difference by the number of months expressed in tenths of a year above the lower limit of the Range of Child's Age in table ($.3 \times 1.4 = .42$).
  c. Add this product to the lower limit of the Range of Child's XGE in table ($7.4 + .42 = 7.82$ or 7.8). Therefore, the XGE for a child who is 11.3 years of age with an IQ of 119 is 7.8. Steps a, b, and c may also be used to find the XGE for +.5 of a year.

The Expectancy Scores Table was based upon the following formulae devised by Alice Horn (6) (go to page 54):

Expectancy Scores

I Q	Grades 1 (Age 6–0)	2 (Age 7–0)	3 (Age 8–0)	4 (Age 9–0)	5 (Age 10–0)	6 (Age 11–0)	7 (Age 12–0)	8 (Age 13–0)
70	K.1	1.0	1.8	2.4	3.0	3.8	4.3	5.1
71	K.2	1.0	1.9	2.4	3.1	3.9	4.4	5.2
72	K.2	1.1	1.9	2.5	3.1	3.9	4.5	5.3
73	K.2	1.0	2.0	2.5	3.2	4.0	4.6	5.4
74	K.3	1.1	2.0	2.6	3.3	4.1	4.7	5.5
75	K.3	1.2	2.0	2.7	3.4	4.2	4.8	5.6
76	K.3	1.2	2.1	2.7	3.4	4.2	4.9	5.7
77	K.4	1.2	2.1	2.8	3.5	4.4	5.0	5.8
78	K.3	1.2	2.1	2.8	3.6	4.4	5.1	5.9
79	K.4	1.3	2.2	2.9	3.6	4.5	5.2	6.0
80	K.4	1.3	1.2	2.9	3.7	4.6	5.2	6.1
81	K.4	1.3	2.2	3.0	3.7	4.6	5.3	6.2
82	K.5	1.4	2.3	3.0	3.8	4.7	5.4	6.3
83	K.5	1.5	2.4	3.1	3.9	4.8	5.5	6.4
84	K.6	1.5	2.4	3.1	3.9	4.8	5.6	6.5
85	K.6	1.5	2.4	3.2	4.0	4.9	5.7	6.6
86	K.6	1.6	2.5	3.2	4.1	5.0	5.7	6.6
87	K.7	1.6	2.5	3.3	4.1	5.0	5.8	6.7
88	K.7	1.6	2.6	3.6	4.2	5.1	5.9	6.8
89	K.7	1.7	2.6	3.4	4.3	5.2	6.0	6.9
90	K.7	1.7	2.6	3.5	4.4	5.3	6.1	7.0
91	K.8	1.7	2.7	3.5	4.4	5.3	6.2	7.2
92	K.8	1.8	2.7	3.6	4.5	5.5	6.3	7.3
93	K.8	1.8	2.8	3.6	4.6	5.5	6.4	7.4
94	K.9	1.8	2.8	3.7	4.6	5.6	6.5	7.5

51

Expectancy Scores—(cont.)

I Q	*Grades* 1 (Age 6–0)	2 (Age 7–0)	3 (Age 8–0)	4 (Age 9–0)	5 (Age 10–0)	6 (Age 11–0)	7 (Age 12–0)	8 (Age 13–0)
95	K.9	1.9	2.8	3.7	4.7	5.7	6.6	7.6
96	K.9	1.9	2.9	3.8	4.7	5.7	6.6	7.6
97	1.0	1.9	2.9	3.8	4.8	5.8	6.7	7.7
98	1.0	1.9	2.9	3.9	4.9	5.9	6.8	7.8
99	1.0	2.0	3.0	3.9	4.9	5.9	6.9	7.9
100	1.0	2.0	3.0	4.0	5.0	6.0	7.0	8.0
101	1.0	2.0	3.0	4.1	5.1	6.1	7.1	8.1
102	1.1	2.1	3.1	4.1	5.1	6.1	7.2	8.2
103	1.1	2.2	3.2	4.2	5.2	6.2	7.3	8.3
104	1.2	2.2	3.2	4.2	5.3	6.3	7.4	8.4
105	1.2	2.2	3.2	4.3	5.4	6.4	7.5	8.5
106	1.2	2.3	3.3	4.3	5.4	6.4	7.6	8.6
107	1.3	2.3	3.3	4.4	5.5	6.6	7.7	8.7
108	1.3	2.3	3.4	4.4	5.6	6.6	7.8	8.8
109	1.3	2.4	3.4	4.5	5.6	6.7	7.9	8.9
110	1.3	2.4	3.4	4.5	5.7	6.8	7.9	9.0
111	1.4	2.4	3.5	4.6	5.7	6.8	8.0	9.1
112	1.4	2.5	3.5	4.6	5.8	6.9	8.1	9.2
113	1.4	2.5	3.6	4.7	5.9	7.0	8.2	9.3
114	1.5	2.5	3.6	4.8	5.9	7.0	8.3	9.4
115	1.5	2.6	3.6	4.8	6.0	7.1	8.4	9.5
116	1.5	2.6	3.7	4.9	6.1	7.2	8.5	9.6
117	1.6	2.6	3.7	4.9	6.1	7.2	8.6	9.7
118	1.5	2.6	3.7	5.0	6.2	7.3	8.7	9.8
119	1.6	2.7	3.8	5.0	6.3	7.4	8.8	9.9

52

Expectancy Scores—(cont.)

I Q	Grades 1 (Age 6–0)	2 (Age 7–0)	3 (Age 8–0)	4 (Age 9–0)	5 (Age 10–0)	6 (Age 11–0)	7 (Age 12–0)	8 (Age 13–0)
120	1.6	2.7	3.8	5.1	6.4	7.5	8.8	9.9
121	1.6	2.7	3.8	5.1	6.4	7.5	8.9	10.1
122	1.7	2.8	3.9	5.2	6.5	7.7	9.0	10.2
123	1.7	2.9	4.0	5.2	6.6	7.7	9.1	10.3
124	1.8	2.9	4.0	5.3	6.6	7.8	9.2	10.4
125	1.8	2.9	4.0	5.4	6.7	7.9	9.3	10.5
126	1.8	3.0	4.1	5.4	6.7	7.9	9.3	10.5
127	1.9	3.0	4.1	5.5	6.8	8.0	9.4	10.6
128	1.9	3.0	4.2	5.5	6.9	8.1	9.5	10.7
129	1.9	3.1	4.2	5.6	6.9	8.1	9.6	10.8
130	1.9	3.1	4.2	5.6	7.0	8.2	9.7	10.9
131	2.0	3.1	4.3	5.7	7.1	8.3	9.8	11.1
132	2.0	3.2	4.3	5.7	7.1	8.3	9.9	11.2
133	2.0	3.2	4.4	5.8	7.2	8.4	10.0	11.3
134	2.1	3.2	4.4	5.8	7.3	8.5	10.1	11.4
135	2.1	3.3	4.4	5.9	7.4	8.6	10.2	11.5
136	2.1	3.3	4.5	5.9	7.4	8.6	10.2	11.5
137	2.2	3.3	4.5	6.0	7.5	8.8	10.3	11.6
138	2.1	3.3	4.5	6.1	7.6	8.8	10.4	11.7
139	2.2	3.4	4.6	6.1	7.6	8.9	10.5	11.8
140	2.2	3.4	4.6	6.2	7.7	9.0	10.6	11.9

53

Child's Present Age	Horn's Formula
6.0–8.5	$\dfrac{MA + CA}{2}$
8.6–9.11	$\dfrac{3\,MA + 2\,CA}{5}$
10.0–11.11	$\dfrac{2\,MA + CA}{3}$
12 and above	$\dfrac{3\,MA + CA}{4}$

NOTE: For those wishing to compute XGEs instead of using the table, to convert the child's age to months in the IQ formula for finding his MA, use the form $12 \times y + m$, where $y =$ years and $m =$ months.

Example: If 7.1 means seven years and one month, then $12 \times 7 + 1 = 85$ months.

Example: If 7.10 means seven years and ten months, then $12 \times 7 + 10 = 84 + 10 = 94$ months.

In the following chart, Mary, John, and Phillip are underachievers as shown by the expected grade equivalents (XGE) for each child. These computations have been done as additional examples for the reader.

Child	*IQ*	*Age*	*Grade Score on Achievement Test*	*XGE*	*Under-achiever*
Mary	131	8.6	3.2	5.1	✓
June	123	8.6	3.9	4.7	
Bill	89	10.7	4.0	4.9	
John	115	7.2	1.7	2.8	✓
Phillip	108	10.2	4.2	5.8	✓

Note: Appreciation is expressed to Colleen Hartley, special education teacher, Riverside, Calif., for identifying a need for the Expectancy Scores Table, and to Joe Hartley, law student, University of Wisconsin, for producing the computer program and print out of the table.

8

Some Other Tools for Diagnostic Teaching

The more evidence that is obtained for diagnosing learning difficulties, the better your chances for helping the child. Perhaps the learning difficulty stems from a lack of readiness. Maybe the task to be performed by the child is too difficult for her level of learning. Previous instruction may have been inappropriate. Evidence should be obtained in all of these areas: the child, the task, and the instruction. The following chapter includes some ways of tapping these three areas.

The Child's Readiness: Piagetian Tasks

The Swiss psychologist Jean Piaget has provided activities for observing whether a child has acquired various concepts basic to understanding the meaning of numbers(7). Here are a few of Piaget's activities:

One-to-One Correspondence

Place six raisins in a row: o o o o o o. Say, "Can you make another row that has the same number of raisins in it as this one?"

Or, in another activity, place six paper cups before the child in a row. Say, "Pretend that you are giving a party. You have cups for your party, but you need a napkin for each cup. Take these napkins (hand child about fifteen napkins) and give each cup a napkin." The child then is to match up a napkin for each cup and recognize that she does not need to use some of the napkins. Failure on these last two tasks implies a lack of the one-to-one correspondence which is a necessary prerequisite to number work.

Conservation of Number—A

Sit across a table from a child. Place two rows of objects (raisins, clay balls, crunched up pieces of paper, pennies, etc.), with six objects in each row, between you and the child. Place the objects in each row equidistant from each other so that both rows are the same length. Say to the child, "Are there the same number of _____ (name the object) in both rows?"

> Row A   o o o o o o
> Row B   o o o o o o

If the child agrees that there are the same number in both rows, you may continue with the exercise. If she does not, stop here because she already has shown a lack of readiness for number concepts.

Next, spread the row of six objects out so that one row is longer than the other, although the number of both rows remains the same. Say again "Are there the same number of _____ (name of the objects) in both rows?"

> Row A   o o o o o o
> Row B   o   o   o   o   o   o

Be careful not to help or hinder the child in her answer by using cue words. For example, *do not* say, "Are there the same number of _____ in both rows *now?*" The word *now* may indicate that a change in number has occurred. Also, *do not* say, "Are both rows the same?" The child may be thinking of the absolute meaning for the word *same* instead of the relative meaning. The absolute meaning implies equality (only one row would be involved), while it is the relative meaning that implies equivalence (two rows having the same number of objects).

You are interested in whether the child can focus on the equivalence of the two rows rather than on the length of the rows. Children under five years of age usually respond, "There are more in the stretched out row;" they are being fooled by their perception.

Piaget would say that they are nonconservers of number. They begin to be conservers at the middle or end of their fifth year, and by the end of their eighth year, most are able to do this task. Before a child can compare equivalent sets and tell which sets have a particular number of objects, she must be able to observe the number property of a set without being distracted by color of objects, size, or spatial arrangements.

Conservation of Number—B

Place two rows of objects between you and the child, with six objects in each row and both rows the same length. Repeat the above question, "Are there the same number of _____ in both rows?"

Row A: o o o o o o
Row B: o o o o o o

Next, add objects to Row B without changing the length of either row.

Row A: o o o o o o
Row B: oooooooooo

You now have changed the density of Row B, while leaving the endpoints equidistant. Repeat the question "Are there the same number of _____ in both rows?"

Conservation of Number—C
(Discontinuous Quantity)

Show the child two paper cups, each containing fifteen marbles. Ask the child, "Are there the same number of marbles in each cup?" If there is doubt, let her count the marbles. Then pour the marbles from one cup into a shallow pan. Ask, "Are there the same number of marbles in the cup and the pan?"

If the child is able to identify the fact that the number of marbles does not change even though the spatial arrangement of one set of marbles is more spread out, then the child is said to be a conserver of number. She is looking at the number property of the set and is not fooled by perceptual changes.

Piaget also talks about "reversibility" as a necessary component of conservation (*8*). By this, he means that the child is able to think, "There were the same number of marbles in both cups before the marbles in one cup were poured into the pan. If I were to pour the marbles from the pan back into the cup, I could see that the number of marbles in both cups would be the same again. So, since I can reverse the operation, the number of marbles does not change whether they are in the cup or in the pan."

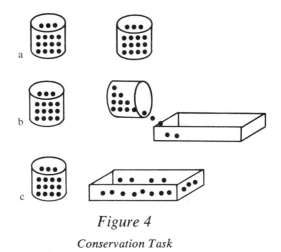

Figure 4

Conservation Task

In his mind's eye, the child is able to reverse the appearance of the marbles in the pan to their previous appearance in the cup. This ability aids the child to ignore the change in appearance of the marbles; when she has developed this skill, she will attend to the number property and not to the spatial arrangement of the marbles. This activity involves the concept of "identity." The set of marbles in the cup is the same set of marbles in the pan; therefore, the number property logically must be the same regardless of appearance. Success in this activity facilitates an understanding of addition, subtraction, multiplication, and division.

Serial Correspondence

Use straws of different lengths for this exercise. Say, "Can you make a staircase with these straws?" The child here is demonstrating a readiness for arranging objects in a specific order (from smallest to largest or from largest to smallest). Next, you might show the child sets of objects and ask her to arrange them in a certain order. For example, present sets of objects ranging in number from two to six. Say, "Which set has the smallest number of objects?" Guide the child to point to the set with two objects. Continue in this manner until all sets have been moved in a left-to-right alteration of smallest to largest, increasing by one object each time.

When the child is able to arrange sets of objects from smallest to largest with guidance, change your procedure to give the child less guidance. Give her five sets having from two to six objects and simply say, "Arrange these sets of objects in order from the smallest to the largest in number.

You may vary your instructions by asking that the sets be arranged from largest to smallest in number. Also, you may present only even numbered (or odd numbered) sets and guide the child to arrange these in some order.

These activities provide a diagnostic profile of your student's readiness for number work. They are especially helpful in grades kindergarten, one, two, and three.

Children in kindergarten and grade one are developing one-to-one correspondence, many-to-one correspondence, conservation of number (the lasting equivalence of corresponding sets), seriation (ordering of sets), reversibility (ability to perceive mentally the original condition of a set of objects) (8), and identifying (the concept of "absolute sameness" where a set of objects is moved in either space or time; the set may undergo a change in location from a cup to a pan or it may be considered to exist both now and ten minutes from now).

Usually by grades two or three, these relationships are demonstrable. If a child in grade two or three is not able to perform these conservation activities, she may need quantitative experiences at the concrete level as prerequisites to performing mathematical computations which are at the symbolic level. Failure to perform these conservation tasks at these ages may also be indicative of a slower rate of cognitive development.

The Meaning of the Task

The teacher must be able to identify the specific desired learning and the conditions necessary for this type of learning to occur. William Brownell and Gordon Hendrickson have presented a model which helps to determine the kind of learning involved in a particular learning task(2). They place learning products on a continuum of meaning.

$$(\text{zero}) \quad 0 \ldots \text{———} \ldots N \quad (\text{maximum})$$

Knowledge which has a minimum of meaningful value would fall toward the zero end of the scale. For example, the numeral 2 is a label just as is the word *two* and has no rational explanation; it was selected arbitrarily. The letter d follows c and precedes e; once again, there is a minimum of meaning. However, the addition fact "$2 + 2 = 4$" moves toward the N part of the continuum. Involved here is the idea of "twoness," of "fourness," an understanding of equivalence ($=$), and an understanding of addition ($+$). Although $2 + 2 = 4$ often is referred to as an addition "fact," it is instead a relational combination of concepts that Brownell labels *generalizations*.

Brownell and Hendrickson discuss four types of learning in their model: arbitrary association, concepts, generalizations or principles, and problem solving.

Arbitrary Associations. These are facts which have no meaning. For instance, the fact that the numeral 2 stands for the number *two* is a man-made agreement which aids communication. When you see the numeral 2, you know it represents this many: xx. Another example is the word

table which stands for the physical model of a table . Success

in learning arbitrary associations is usually measured by the correctness and the quickness of the response.

Concepts. These are abstractions and must be taught through appropriate experiences "with consideration given to the learner's background, interests, attitudes dealing with errors, motivation, and learning activities that he has already experienced"(*11*). In discussing the retention of a learned concept, Brownell suggests the importance of encouraging the student to put the concept to use. In such cases, the method of instruction may have been effective, but the infrequent use of the concept may be the diagnosed reason for difficulty in his learning.

In learning basic mathematical concepts, it is important for the child to have motor experiences. Just as one cannot really get the idea of "hammer" without using a hammer, a child needs to manipulate sets of objects to abstract the number property of the set.

As an exercise, present a child with two sets of five objects and guide her to match these sets to one another on a one-to-one basis. First, give her two sets having the same objects (red blocks, yellow circles, white straws, etc.) and direct that she tell you what is the same about both sets. She may say that both sets have "blocks," that they both contain "red blocks," that the blocks are "made of wood," or that they both contain "five" blocks in each set.

Next, present a set of five red plastic straws. Say, "Now tell me what is the same about these three sets?" The child may say all three have "red things" and each set has five objects.

Then present a set of five yellow paper circles. Notice that the straws are plastic so that the only attribute that is now the same for all four sets is the number property: "fiveness." Ask the child to tell you what is the same about all four sets. She should say, "They all have five objects."

This sequence of experiences allows the child to attend to similar attributes: color, shape, size, and—finally—number. It is a process whereby the number concept is abstracted. The child now has a grasp of what "fiveness" means. She has actively used her senses of sight, touch, smell, hearing, and—perhaps—even taste to determine what was the same about the sets of five.

This abstraction process involves the child's ability to classify. If you wish to determine whether or not the child can classify, you might use the activity with the four sets just described and observe the child's answers. If the child is able to tell you what is the same about the sets, she is showing that she is able to classify.

An alternate procedure for diagnosing a child's ability to abstract the number concept of sets involves a motor response. Instead of her verbally telling you what is the same about two or more sets, have the child do the following:

1. Show a set of five red blocks. Then give the child a set of six red blocks and say, "You make a set that is the same as the set I made." If the child uses all of the red blocks, she is not attending to the number property. Tell her you see something that is not the same about both sets. Say, "Can you change something in your set to make it more like mine?" Do not ask for a change unless the child sees that she has one too many blocks.

2. Now bring forth a set of five red plastic straws and move your set of five red blocks away from the child's set of blocks and the set of straws, but still keep all three sets in the child's view. Say, "If you know something the same about your set (the five red blocks) and the straws, then move your set closer to the straws." The child may be responding to either color or number (if she matches only five blocks to the five straws) at this level. You need to present one more set to focus on just the number concept.

3. Move the set of straws aside and display a set of five yellow paper circles. Say, "If you know something about your set (child needed to select only the five red blocks by now or should have stopped at Step 2) that is the same as this set (circles), then move your set closer to the new set." At this point, you have eliminated the attributes of shape, color, material, size, and function of object; only the common number property remains.

4. In Steps 1–3, there has been no need for verbal communication. As a diagnostic check, you now might say, "What is the *one thing* that is the same about all of these sets?" The child should say, "They all have the same number of objects."

When the child is able to abstract the number properties of sets, she is able to form relationships between two numbers. For example, she discovers that "threeness plus fiveness" are "eightness." She has formed a relationship between two concepts and that is known as a *generalization*.

Generalizations. These state relationships between or among two or more concepts. For example: $3 + 5 = 8$ is a generalization because the concepts three and five are combined by the addition relation. Generalizations are tools for problem solving.

Problem solving. This type of learning is initiated by a problem. Its success depends on a firm background of arbitrary associations, concepts, and generalizations. For example, in verbal problem solving in mathematics, the child needs to be able to perform the addition relation on the number concepts in order to solve the problem, "Mary has three red pencils and five blue pencils; how many pencils does she have altogether?"

Implications for Instruction

Brownell suggests that when you can identify whether your student is learning an arbitrary association, a concept, a generalization, or is problem solving, you are better able to decide what method of instruction to use.

Basically, there are two methods of instruction: the teacher tells (didactic method) or the student discovers (guided discovery method).

Arbitrary associations cannot be discovered. They are man-made agreements and must be transmitted by "telling." However, concepts and generalizations lend themselves well to guided discovery teaching (the abstracting of the number five described above was presented in a guided discovery manner).

Since problem solving embodies arbitrary associations, concepts, and generalizations, it involves some telling and some discovery. Thus, the teacher must diagnose what type of learning (arbitrary association, concept, or generalization) is involved and determine the conditions necessary for its being learned. The following are examples of mathematics curricula that have been categorized according to Brownell's hierarchy of types of learning:

Example: $3 + 5 = \Box$

Type of Learning: Generalization (Principle)

Example: Draw a circle around the sets with five objects.

```
X          X X          X X          X  X X          X X X
                                        X                X X
  X                                   
              X X          X          X     X
  X                        
                           X X
```

Type of Learning: Concept

Example: Write the numeral to show three objects are in the set.

```
X X
  X        _____
```

Type of Learning: Arbitrary Association

Example: $7 \times 3 = 3 \times \square$

Type of Learning: Generalization (Principle)

Example: State the axiom underlying the following examples.

$$7 \times 3 = 3 \times 7 \quad _____$$
$$4 + 6 = 6 + 4 \quad _____$$

Type of Learning: Generalization or Principle Learning

Gagne's Hierarchy of Types of Learning*

Another tool for diagnosing the type of learning with which the student is involved has been proposed by Robert Gagne (5). Gagne discusses two conditions for learning: internal conditions and external conditions. By internal conditions, he means those capabilities already possessed by the learner. The internal conditions of learning include all behaviors and capabilities that the learner needs for successfully approaching some new level of learning. Learning conditions that are external to the learner

---

* Adapted and reprinted from *The Conditions of Learning,* 2d ed. by Robert M. Gagne (New York: Holt, Rinehart and Winston, Inc., 1965), by permission of the publisher. Copyright © 1965, 1970 by Holt, Rinehart, and Winston, Inc.

include those situations that are outside of him and over which he may not have direct control. It is the external conditions that include those behaviors and activities we call "instruction." Gagne has presented a hierarchy of eight types of learning. He believes that in order for a student to learn a particular learning type (say Type 4), he must perform the skills necessary for Type 3. This hierarchy uses Gagne's notion of "necessary prerequisites" which was discussed on pages 29–36 of this book.

The first two of the eight types of learning are Signal Learning and Stimulus—Response Learning. They represent the most basic forms of learning and provide the base upon which other more complex forms of learning are built.

Type 1—Signal Learning. Signal Learning is synonomous with the "conditioned response" that involves a substitute stimulus accompanying a particular response. The classic example for this learning is Pavlov's experiment in which he substituted the sound of a bell for food powder, which was followed by the flow of saliva in a dog's mouth. The bell (conditioned stimulus) is sounded just before spraying food powder (unconditioned stimulus) into the dog's mouth. The food powder had originally been accompanied by the saliva response (unconditioned response). Then the bell and the food powder are presented in close sequence with the bell preceding a spray of food powder by about one-half second, and the dog salivates. Finally, the bell alone is sounded and the saliva is emitted as shown below:

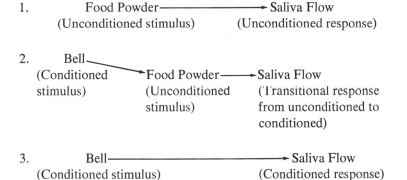

1. Food Powder ⟶ Saliva Flow
    (Unconditioned stimulus) (Unconditioned response)

2. Bell ⟶ Food Powder ⟶ Saliva Flow
    (Conditioned stimulus) (Unconditioned stimulus) (Transitional response from unconditioned to conditioned)

3. Bell ⟶ Saliva Flow
    (Conditioned stimulus) (Conditioned response)

Step 2 is really a learning process. After the series of Bell ⟶ Food Powder was repeated a few times, the signal or conditioned stimulus (bell) was accompanied by a learned response (the saliva flow) without the food powder.

Internal conditions for Type 1 learning involve natural reflexes, such as eye blink and salivation, and reflexive emotional responses including fear, anger, or pleasure on the part of the learner.

The two external conditions for signal learning are contiguity of stimuli and repetition. Contiguity in this sense means that both the signal and the unconditioned stimulus must be presented in close proximity to each other. The amount of repetition needed varies with the situation.

In applying this type of learning to teaching mathematics, consider the child's past experiences in learning mathematics. If success has been minimal or altogether lacking, a sick feeling may have been felt by the learner. In later grades, this same sick feeling may occur in response to the very request, "Take out your math books." Thus, it is important to investigate your student's past experiences in learning mathematics, for such investigation may throw light on present difficulties.

Type 2—Stimulus—Response Learning. This differs from Type 1 in that the first type is concerned with reflexive responses over which the individual has little control. Type 2 learning emphasizes a single connection between some stimulus situation and some response situation. It is trial-and-error learning in which the first responses eventually are funneled to the desired outcome by rewarding only those responses that approximate the desired response.

The internal condition for Type 2 learning is the ability of the learner to make the learned response; the terminating response must provide satisfaction or reinforcement to the learner. The external conditions for Type 2 learning are contiguity and reinforcement. Withholding reinforcement results in the disappearance or extinction of the response.

An example of Type 2 learning may be a child's responding to flash cards. For example hold up $\overset{5}{+3}$ (stimulus); child responds "eight;" you smile, nod your head, and present another flash card (reinforcement). This does not necessarily imply that the child has any meaning for the stimulus. In fact, when flash cards are used prematurely in mathematics classes (that is, prior to the child's abstracting the number idea), the rote learning that occurs is Type 2 learning.

Another example of Type 2 learning involves the child's learning arbitrary associations. For instance, the child learns the names of numerals [1 ("One"), 2 ("Two"), 6 ("Six")] in a stimulus-response situation. The child is presented the numeral and responds with the numeral's name.

At a higher grade level, learning the names of the axioms exemplifies Type 2 learning. A student's learning the name "Commutative Property for Addition" may only approximate the correct response, but through repetition and reinforcement, the teacher finally guides him to the correct verbal response.

Type 3—Chaining. Chaining involves motor behavior. It implies that there is a series of motor acts in which the actions are connected one to the next. For the task to be successful, each individual $S \longrightarrow R$ link must be performed correctly and in the right order. It is essential that the learner be able to perform the individual acts (e.g., opening a door).

The internal conditions of chaining involve the previous learning of each stimulus-response connection and the presence of kinesthetic feedback. The external conditions of Type 3 learning are getting the learner to sequence the links in a particular order, putting the links in close time succession (contiguity), repetition, and reinforcement. The first external condition, establishing the proper order of the links, may be accomplished in two ways. You may begin with the terminal link and work backwards, or you may start at the beginning and work toward the end of the chain with verbal prompting to guide the learner.

Examples of chaining are using scissors, catching balls, touch typing, buttoning, using a pencil, unlocking a door with a key, and starting an engine. So far as teaching mathematics, an example of chaining is a child's ability to write the numerals from 1 through 9 forming each correctly.

Type 4—Verbal Association. This type of learning involves naming or labeling. Degree of meaning is not a part of verbal associations.

The internal conditions of Verbal Associations learning are the same as for Type 3. Each link in the Association must have been learned previously as an $S \longrightarrow R$ connection. The external conditions include presenting the verbal units in proper sequence, actively involving the learner in the responding, providing confirmation of correct responses, and reinforcing these correct responses.

Examples of Type 4 learning are memorizing telephone numbers and poems, reciting the alphabet, and rote saying of multiplication tables.

Type 5—Multiple Discrimination Learning. This type involves discrimination tasks such as distinguishing shape, color, texture, words, numerals.

The internal conditions for Type 5 learning consist of the learner's having acquired the four lower types. For example, if the learner is expected to discriminate between the numeral *3* and the capital letter *E,* she must have learned previously to associate the name verbally with its written character. The external conditions consist of prompting or cues, repetition, positive reinforcement, and the use of real or construction paper objects. In the beginning stages of the multiple discrimination task, the chains must be presented one at a time until the student knows them. Unless the learner knows the objects (or in some cases concepts) to be discriminated, she has no basis for comparing and selecting attributes for discrimination. Unless the child *knows* the numeral *3* and the capital letter *E,* she may not be expected to discriminate between them. Unless she has already acquired the concept "yellowness," "greenness," and "blueness," she will not be able to select objects similar in color to form sets as in the tasks which follow. Thus, it appears that there is a circularity to the hierarchy. Here is an instance when what appears to be a higher type learning is, at closer look, prerequisite to a lower type learning.

For a child to perform a discrimination task such as selecting a yellow object from assorted color objects, he or she must already have acquired the concept "yellow." How, otherwise, can a child hand you a yellow object? This may be considered an internal condition according to this theory. However, in diagnostic teaching, internal conditions may not be assumed. In fact, the identification of such a missing "internal condition" may well be the key to the remediation-instruction component of the diagnostic teaching cycle.

In applying Type 5 learning to teaching mathematics, an example is set discrimination. Present a child with a group of objects, such as four yellow circles, two green squares, two blue squares, four green triangles, and four yellow straws.

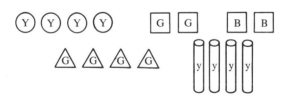

Figure 5

Discrimination Task

Now, present the child with tasks in regard to the following attributes:

Attribute 1—Color: Ask the child to make *three* sets with these objects so that all members of a set are the same color.

Response:

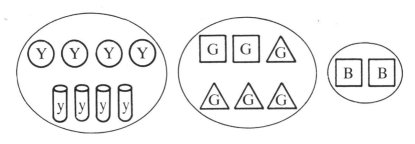

Figure 6

Discrimination Task—Color

Attribute 2—Shape: Say, "Make *four* sets so that all members of a set have the same shape."

Response:

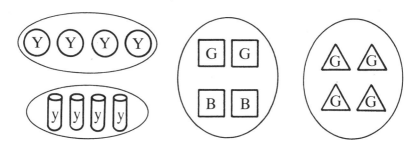

Figure 7

Discrimination Task—Shape

Attribute 3—Function: Given a pencil, a penny, and a block, say to the child, "Hand me the object you can write with."

Other examples of Type 5 learning are identifying different numerals, having the child select her coat from among others, or selecting a square blue object from other colors and shapes.

Type 6—Concept Learning. Concept learning involves the meaningful labeling of a class of objects. The focus here is on abstracting similarities among objects in a set. The grouping of different sized circles and labeling them "circles" is an example of concept learning.

The internal conditions are the same as those established in Type 5 learning. External conditions include presenting stimulus objects simultaneously, cueing or prompting to aid the learner in identifying the common link in the stimulus situation, and reinforcement of correct responses.

Examples of concept learning include the fact that whales, dogs, cats are mammals, and understanding that the numerals 1, 2, 3, 7, 9 are symbols which represent numbers.

In mathematics teaching, the following are examples of testing for Type 6 learning:

1. Draw a circle around the even number.

   Response: 3 5 ⑥ 7 9

2. Draw a circle around the sets that show the number six.

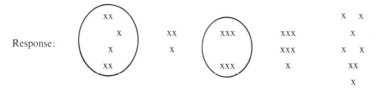

3. What number is represented in the place value chart?

tens	ones
	xx

   Response: "two."

4. Make *two* sets so that both sets have the same number of objects."

   Response:

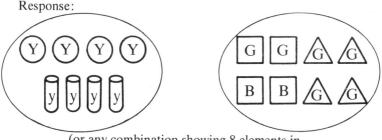

   (or any combination showing 8 elements in a set).

Figure 8

Concept Learning—Cardinality

Type 7—Principle Learning. A principle is a relational combination of two or more concepts. The internal condition is that the learner already knows the concepts which make up the principle. For example, in the principle *round things roll,* the concepts *round* and *things* must be within the learner's conceptual structure as does the meaning of the relationship *roll.*

The external conditions include the following:

1. Give the learner an explanation of the behavior expected. For example,

   "I want you to answer the question, what kinds of things roll?"

2. Question the learner so that she must recall the previously learned concepts.

   "Show me what things mean."
   "Pick out the round objects."

3. Use verbal statements that will lead the learner to put the principle together as a chain of concepts in the proper order.

   "Do all round things roll?"

4. By means of a question, ask the learner to demonstrate concrete instances of the principle.

   "Can you show me that all the round things roll?"

5. By the use of a suitable question, require the learner to make a verbal statement of the principle.

   "What kinds of things roll?"

Gagne presents evidence that the learning of high level principles is dependent upon the mastery of prerequisite low level principles. Examples of principles in teaching elementary school mathematics are:

Commutative Property for Addition (CPA).
   For every two numbers, a and b:

$$a + b = b + a$$
$$3 + 8 = 8 + 3$$

Commutative Property for Multiplication (CPM).
   For every two numbers, a and b:

$$a \times b = b \times a$$
$$3 \times 8 = 8 \times 3$$

Associative Property for Addition (APA).
For every three numbers, a, b, and c:
$$a + (b + c) = (a + b) + c$$
$$3 + (4 + 5) = (3 + 4) + 5$$

Associative Property for Multiplication (APM).
For every three numbers a, b, and c:
$$a \times (b \times c) = (a \times b) \times c$$
$$3 \times (4 \times 5) = (3 \times 4) \times 5$$

Distributive Property for Multiplication over Addition (DPMA).
For every three numbers a, b, and c:
$$a \times (b + c) = (a \times b) + (a \times c)$$
$$4 \times (5 + 6) = (4 \times 5) + (4 \times 6)$$

Additive Inverse.
A number added to its inverse sums to zero.
$$4 + (-4) = 0$$

Multiplicative Inverse.
A number multiplied by its inverse yields the number one.
$$\frac{2}{3} \times \frac{3}{2} = \frac{6}{6} = 1$$

Identity Principle for Addition.
For every number a:
$$a + 0 = a$$
$$87 + 0 = 87$$

Identity Principle for Multiplication.
For every number a:
$$a \times 1 = a$$
$$87 \times 1 = 87$$

Principle for Multiplying by 0.
For every number a:
$$a \times 0 = 0$$
$$87 \times 0 = 0$$

Type 8—Problem Solving. The learner uses principles to succeed in a problem situation. As learning goes on, higher order principles emerge from the problem-solving situation. Problem solving involves four steps:

1. Presentation of the problem.
2. Definition of the problem; this step distinguishes the essential features in a situation.
3. Formulation of hypotheses.
4. Verification of hypotheses.

Conditions within the learner include the learner's ability to recall those principles learned previously which are relevant to her solving of the present problem. External conditions for Type 8 learning must provide for recall of the relevant principles so that these may be organized by the learner to achieve a solution. Verbal cues are provided to help guide the learner to the solution.

Examples of problem solving in teaching elementary school mathematics include verbal problem solving as well as discovery situations.

Example A: Mary has seven more dresses than her sister. If her sister has ten, how many dresses does Mary have?

Necessary prerequisites:

1. Learner reads the problem.
2. Learner analyzes verbal problem to select what information is given and what is wanted (*14*).

Given	*Wanted*
Sister has ten dresses.	
Mary has seven more.	
	Number of dresses Mary has = ☐

3. Learner translates verbal sentence into mathematical sentence.

$$10 \quad \triangle \quad 7 = \square$$

At this point, the child must decide on the appropriate mathematical operation (addition, multiplication, subtraction, division) to solve the problem. Guide the learner by asking about the wanted—given situation. If the wanted is a *whole* and the *parts* are given, then the operation will be either addition or multiplication. On the other hand, if the wanted is the unknown *part* and the given contains the *whole and known part,* then the appropriate operation is either subtraction or division. The meaning of the verbal problem is a clue for the learner to use in discriminating between which combining operation to use $(+, \times)$ or between which separating operation to use $(-, \div)$. The hardest part for the learner is deciding whether to use a combining or a separation operation. Once this decision is made, learners do not seem to have trouble deciding which operation within the combining or separating category to select.

In the example above, we are given the parts and want a whole. The obvious operation to use here is addition.

$$10 + 7 = \square$$

4. Finds solution. $\qquad 17 = \square$

Example B: Discovery problem-solving situation. Present child with paper circular region and a ruler. Ask her to find the length of the distance around the circle (circumference).

Necessary prerequisites:

1. Child can use a ruler properly.
2. Child's motor skills are developed to point where she can handle the circle, the ruler, and other objects such as string, pencils, etc.

Solution 1: Child may obtain a piece of string, shoelace, or belt and place it around the circular region. Then she can measure the part of the string that went around the circle with a ruler. This is an indirect measure of the circle's circumference.

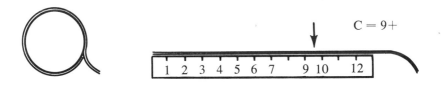

Figure 9

Indirect Measure of Circumference

Solution 2: Child may mark a point on edge of circle and roll it along ruler until point again touches ruler.

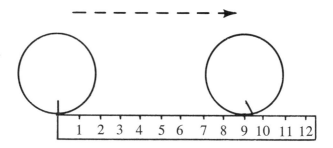

Figure 10

Measuring Circumference

Solution 3: Child may place the circle between two pencils. The distance between the two pencils then may be measured on the ruler. If the child knows the formula $C = \Pi d$, she can find the measure of the circumference by plugging $\frac{22}{7}$ or 3.14 into the formula for "Π," substituting the measure of the diameter for "d," and multiplying.

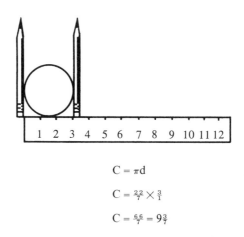

$$C = \pi d$$
$$C = \tfrac{22}{7} \times \tfrac{3}{1}$$
$$C = \tfrac{66}{7} = 9\tfrac{3}{7}$$

Figure 11

Formula for Finding Circumference

By using Gagne's hierarchy of eight types of learning and Brownell's idea of the four levels of learning to identify the nature of the content to be taught, you can then decide upon the most appropriate method of instruction.

If you classify the content at the arbitrary association level in Brownell's scheme, you know that there is a minimum of meaning inbedded in what is to be taught. However, principle and problem-solving learning are saturated with meaning. The diagram on page 74 will help you visualize the connection between the level of learning and the more appropriate method of instruction. Notice how Gagne's hierarchy matches up with Brownell's. Also, remember that this is a continuum which implies degrees of meaning and degrees of methodology rather than extremes.

Cognitive Domain Taxonomy

The final tool to be presented for use in dealing with intellectual aspects of diagnostic teaching is editor Benjamin Bloom's *Taxonomy of Behavioral Objectives: Cognitive Domain (1)*. This tool is "intended to provide for a classification of the goals of our educational system." Its authors define *cognitive* as including "activities such as remembering and recalling knowledge, thinking, problem-solving, creating."

Included in this taxonomy are knowledge, comprehension, application, analysis, synthesis, and evaluation. These categories are useful tools for creating test questions or evaluative experiences for students of elementary school mathematics.

Knowledge involves recall of material stored in one's memory. It can be categorized as follows:

1.00 Knowledge

    1.10 Knowledge of Specifics

        1.11 Knowledge of Terminology
        1.12 Knowledge of Specific Facts

    1.20 Knowledge of Ways and Means of Dealing with Specifics

        1.21 Knowledge of Conventions
        1.22 Knowledge of Trends and Sequences
        1.23 Knowledge of Classifications and Categories
        1.24 Knowledge of Criteria
        1.25 Knowledge of Methodology

    1.30 Knowledge of the Universals and Abstractions in a Field

        1.31 Knowledge of Principles and Generalizations
        1.32 Knowledge of Theories and Structures

Comprehension comprises the individual's knowing what is being presented and using it without being able to tie the new learning to other learning. This category is classified as follows:

Figure 12

*Continuum of Meaning and Methodology**

* Adapted from "How Children Learn Information, Concepts and Generalizations." In *The 49th Yearbook of the National Society for the Study of Education*, 1950, by permission of the National Society for the Study of Education.

Use of Didactic or Telling Method of Instruction → Use of Guided Discovery Method of Instruction

Minimum Meaning → Maximum Meaning

Signal Learning — Stimulus Response — Chaining — Verbal Associations — Multiple Discriminations — Concepts — Principles — Problem-Solving

Arbitrary Associations — Concepts — Principles — Problem-Solving

76

2.00 Comprehension

    2.10 Translation
    2.20 Interpretation
    2.30 Extrapolation

3.00 *Application* is the use of learning in concrete situations. There is no further categorization of application.

Analysis involves the breakdown of the learning into its elements so that the relative sequence of these parts becomes apparent. This is similar to Gagne's concept of "learning hierarchies." A further classification is:

4.00 Analysis

    4.10 Analysis of Elements
    4.20 Analysis of Relationships
    4.30 Analysis of Organizational Principles

Synthesis is putting parts together to form a whole that was not previously apparent:

5.00 Synthesis

    5.10 Production of a Unique Communication
    5.20 Production of a Plan or Proposed Set of Operations
    5.30 Derivation of a Set of Abstract Relations

Evaluation is making value judgments concerning such matters as the accuracy (see 6.10 below) of a situation or making judgments according to some criterion (see 6.20):

6.00 Evaluation

    6.10 Judgments in Terms of Internal Evidence
    6.20 Judgments in Terms of External Criteria

In order to present a model for using cognitive domain taxonomies, some exercises typical to elementary school mathematics are listed. Objectives are categorized according to Brownell, Gagne, and Bloom. Also included are Bruner's three modes of curriculum representation: enactive, iconic, and symbolic.

Exercises for Elementary School Mathematics

Activity	Brownell	Gagne	Bruner	Bloom
Identify number property of set	Concept	Concept	Enactive or Iconic	2.00 Comprehension
Identify cardinality of a set of objects	Concept	Concept	Enactive	3.00 Application
Identify sequences of counting numbers by ones, tens, and fives	Principle	Principle (also Verbal Association if little meaning to learner)	Symbolic	1.00 Knowledge 1.30 Knowledge of Universals and Abstractions in a Field
Write numerals 1–9 in sequence	Arbitrary Association	Chaining	Symbolic	1.00 Knowledge of Terminology
Associate numbers with points on a number line	Arbitrary Association	Multiple Discrimination	Iconic	2.00 Comprehension 2.10 Translation
Addition Using Associative Property	Principle	Principle	Symbolic	3.00 Application
Subtraction with Renaming (Borrowing)	Principle	Principle	Symbolic	3.00 Application

Exercises for Elementary School Mathematics—(cont.)

Activity	Brownell	Gagne	Bruner	Bloom
Multiplication using Distributive Property	Principle	Principle	Symbolic	3.00 Application
Multiplication using number line	Principle	Principle	Symbolic and Iconic	2.00 Comprehension 2.10 Translation
Division using separation of a set into equivalent subsets	Problem Solving	Problem Solving	Enactive or Iconic	4.10 Analysis of Elements
Write numerals shown on an abacus	Principle	Principle	Iconic and Symbolic	2.00 Comprehension 2.10 Translation
Use place value notation	Principle	Principle	Symbolic	3.00 Application
Multiply by 100	Principle	Principle	Symbolic	3.00 Application
Addition, no renaming, two-place	Principle	Principle	Symbolic	3.00 Application
Addition, renaming, three-place, zero in addends	Problem Solving	Problem Solving	Symbolic	3.00 Application
Column Addition, ragged columns	Problem Solving	Problem Solving	Symbolic	3.00 Application

79

Exercises for Elementary School Mathematics—(cont.)

Activity	Brownell	Gagne	Bruner	Bloom
Subtract, renaming, zero in minuend (whole)	Problem Solving	Problem Solving	Symbolic	3.00 Application
Multiplication, no renaming, one-place by two- and three-place, zeros	Principle	Principle	Symbolic	3.00 Application
Division, no remainder, one- and two-place ÷ one-place	Principle	Principle	Symbolic	3.00 Application
Division, no remainder, one- and two-place ÷ one-place, zeros	Problem Solving	Problem Solving	Symbolic	3.00 Application
Division, remainder, one- and two-place ÷ one-place	Problem Solving	Problem Solving	Symbolic	3.00 Application
Write sets of equivalent fractions	Principle	Principle	Symbolic	2.10 Comprehension, Translation
Classify objects to form sets	Concept	Multiple Discrimination, Concept	Enactive	4.30 Analysis of Organizational Principles

Exercises for Elementary School Mathematics—(cont.)

Activity	Brownell	Gagne	Bruner	Bloom
Count aloud, one-to-one correspondence lacking	Arbitrary Association	Verbal Chaining	Symbolic	1.00 Knowledge
Enumerate, counting aloud—one-to-one correspondence present, example: counting objects in a set to find cardinality ("howmuchness" of set)	Concept	Concept	Enactive and Symbolic	3.00 Application
Solve verbal problems	Problem Solving	Problem Solving	Symbolic	5.00 Synthesis 5.20 Production of a plan, or proposed set of operations
Translate Base Five numeral to Base Ten numeral	Principle	Principle	Symbolic	2.00 Comprehension 2.10 Translation
Estimate whether one number is $>$, $=$, or $<$ another	Principle	Principle	Symbolic	6.00 Evaluation
Write a number sentence from a word problem	Problem Solving	Problem Solving	Symbolic	2.00 Comprehension 2.10 Translation

81

By analyzing your mathematics objectives in this way, you can determine several things:

1. Are your test items covering the range of Bloom's Taxonomy or are they all at the lowest level, 1.10 Knowledge of Specifics?
2. Are you evaluating only arbitrary associations or are you also including activities which tap the higher levels of learning?
3. Are your evaluations always at the symbolic level or do you include enactive and iconic activities too?
4. Are you aware of the necessary prerequisite learning implicit in an activity? This strategy for thinking will force you to identify these necessary prerequisites.
5. The use of these tools will help you to diagnose gaps in your students' mathematical foundations.
6. These tools will help you to decide what methods and materials are most appropriate for teaching a particular facet of your mathematics curriculum.

9

Diagnosing in the Affective Domain

Emphasis usually is placed on teaching and testing in the cognitive domain, but if you take one look around an elementary school classroom, it soon becomes obvious that we also need to deal with the affective domain. I have seen children become completely disabled, both intellectually and emotionally, following a rebuff from the teacher. Many times the child had pushed the teacher beyond all limits knowing that he was asking for disciplinary measures, but when the discipline came, the child would react with surprise, anger, or complete withdrawal. According to Abraham Maslow (1962) "the healthy child is able to be justifiably angry, self-protecting and self-affirming, i.e., reactive aggression. Presumably, then, a child should learn not only how to control his anger, but also how and when to express it." Maslow has presented a hierarchy of needs which is an excellent diagnostic tool in dealing with children as well as adults. Use of this hierarchy helps to explain children's behavior and teachers' reactions to such behavior.

Maslow's Hierarchy of Needs*

Basic in Maslow's hierarchy are the level of physiological needs. Built upon the physiological needs—in order—are the safety needs, the need

---

* Based on *Motivation and Personality,* "Chapter 4," 2d ed. by Abraham H. Maslow (New York: Harper and Row Publishers, Inc., 1970), by permission of the publisher. Copyright © 1970 by Abraham H. Maslow.

to love and to be loved, the self-esteem needs, and the self-actualization level.

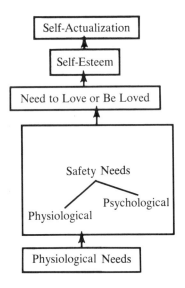

Figure 13

Maslow's Hierarchy of Needs

Physiological Needs

A child who is hungry, cold, ill, terrified, exhausted, or has to go to the bathroom will not be listening to your explanation of prime factors and their relation to multiplication. Such a child would be at Maslow's physiological needs level and probably would not even hear your words. This level is the most basic and must be satisfied before progress to the next level can occur.

Have you ever encountered a situation where you have been reduced to the physiological level? As is the case with all of these needs, it will be helpful if you place yourself on the hierarchy by remembering appropriate situations that you may have been in yourself. The better you understand the feelings one has at the various levels, the more empathy you will have for your students. Instead of taking observable behavior at face value, you will be in a position to diagnose *why* the child is exhibiting a particular behavior. For example, the underachiever often appears academically disabled in a cognitive sense when the trouble really stems from his affective domain.

Unfortunately, there are many children who are hungry when they come to school. I have seen several elementary school children fall sound asleep at their tables or desks amid the noise of a busy classroom. Fortunately, school districts have initiated free or inexpensive breakfast programs for their children. I have talked with teachers who explained that they let a particular child sleep because they had found that the home conditions were not conducive to the child's getting proper amounts of sleep. In one case, parties often went on all night; in another, too many children had to sleep in one bed. This is the real world, and the teacher must be aware of such conditions if he is to effectively reach the children in his care.

Safety Needs

Maslow divided safety needs into two types—physical and psychological.

Physical Safety. An example of a child's not being free to learn because his physical safety need has not been met is exemplified by the youngster who was threatened by his neighborhood gang. The threat "I'm gonna get you" can do much to prevent a child from learning in the classroom. A child in the classroom of a teacher who engages in physical punishment also may live in fear for his physical safety. Children who are physically abused at home are further examples of the physical safety level's not being met.

Psychological Safety. Closely tied to the level of physical need is the psychological safety level. A child sitting in a classroom worrying about the fight his parents had that morning cannot concentrate on academic endeavors. If the child thinks his teacher does not like him, he is not psychologically safe and will have learning difficulties when interacting with this teacher. The first grader who is bussed across town to a strange school in a strange neighborhood will need to develop a feeling of safety before he can be expected to concentrate on academic learning. It is important that the teacher in the receiving school recognize those children who have not satisfied their psychological safety level and aid them in attaining a feeling of personal security.

The Need for Love and the Need to Be Loved

The next need on Maslow's hierarchy deals with love. The child must be able to love himself before he can love others. His self-concept is very much tied up with this level. If the child feels loved, he is free to engage in academic activities. He knows that he will continue to be loved under all circumstances. The child whose parents make him buy love with high grades does not feel satisfied in this need. Many underachievers are performing poorly in school as a result of their need for love not being fulfilled.

The Need for Self-Esteem

This need involves status, recognition, and attention. The peer culture is important in satisfying the need for self-esteem. Many times the child who is not perceived by the teacher as having status in the classroom has a high degree of recognition from his friends. It is important for the teacher to diagnose what activities receive status value among the peer groups. In the 1940s, it was considered "square" for a teen-ager—especially a girl—to obtain high grades in school. The 1960s began a marked change in peer values. In fact, in the area of mathematics, the 1957 Russian Sputnik space shot initiated the development of a high level of esteem for successful mathematics students in the United States.

Self-esteem is a by-product of success. In order to insure that every mathematics student tastes some success, a diagnostic strategy for teaching mathematics is essential. The meshing of the student's cognitive level with the appropriate portion of the task to be learned will help to insure success for the mathematics student. When the child tastes success, he is also experiencing a measure of self-esteem. The teacher recognizes him with words of praise or good grades, and the child has a sense of well-being.

This need may be satisfied at very early ages in academic areas when a diagnostic strategy is employed. The gifted first grader may excel in his mathematics class only if the curriculum is appropriate for his cognitive structure. For instance, there are bright first graders who cannot tell time to the minute. In fact, they may not even be exposed to this skill until third grade. However, when the skill is analyzed and a more appropriate sequence of instruction identified, success can be achieved by the first graders. A feeling of self-esteem is present every time one of these children is asked what time it is and they are able to respond correctly. They will smile and stand up very straight as they receive their praise.

Self-Actualization Level

Maslow considered self-actualization as a "peak experience" occurring mainly in adults. However, I believe that elementary school children can encounter peak experiences. The first-grade children described above who can correctly identify time to the minute appear as though they may have been undergoing a fleeting self-actualizing experience.

When Maslow's hierarchy of needs is used as a tool for diagnosing emotional needs of both student and teacher, increased communication and understanding result. This hierarchy has a great deal of power when applied to parents in an attempt to help them understand their position in relation to their child, who is also your student. The hierarchy helps the teacher to understand his emotional reactions to a student or class and aids the teacher in selecting appropriate behavior when dealing with difficult situations.

Since Maslow's scheme is a hierarchy, prior needs must be satisfied in order to attain a higher level. However, an individual may be at different levels in various subject areas or parts of his life at different times. For example, one minute a student may be at the self-esteem need as he discusses nondecimal numeration systems, and the next he may be reduced to the psychological safety need as a loud clap of thunder of a nearby explosion occurs. An earthquake might lower him to the physical safety need and a severe stomach cramp to the most basic need, the physiological level.

Taxonomy:
Affective Domain*

The Affective Domain Taxonomy helps structure your thinking in diagnosing the attitudes, interests, appreciations, and values of your students in regard to elementary school mathematics. At its lowest level, this hierarchy focuses on the student's awareness of mathematics concepts (is he simply able to perceive them?). Next, it is concerned with his response to mathematics (is he doing something to mathematics?). The third step of the Affective Domain hierarchy involves values (does the student perceive mathematical endeavors as having worth?). At the fourth step, the student organizes his values into some sort of a structure (he looks at the relationships among his values and some emerge as being more important than others). The highest rung on this hierarchy, called *characterization,* involves organizing the interrelationships among values into a philosophy of life (it is at this level that a system of values, beliefs, ideas, and attitudes is created by the student).

---

* This section is based on "Handbook Two: The Affective Domain" of *Taxonomy of Educational Objectives* by Krathwohl, Bloom, and Masia (New York: David McKay and Co., 1964) by permission of the publisher.

Since attitudes and emotions seem to be directly involved in learning mathematics, a diagnostic strategy of teaching mathematics must include awareness of a student's affective domain.

The Affective Domain Taxonomy will clarify levels of emotive behaviors and will help to categorize behavioral objectives dealing with attitudes toward mathematics and with learning this high-status subject. Examples of how to make use of this taxonomy follow:

1.0 Receiving (Attending): Audiovisual devices are helpful in capturing the child's attention at this level, which has three components:

1.1 Awareness
1.2 Willingness to Receive
1.3 Controlled or Selected Attention

An example of Awareness (1.1) is the child who realizes the importance of his identifying what he does not understand in arithmetic, listens more carefully (1.2), and pays particular attention when the teacher reviews his weak area (1.3).

Objectives here might include the development of awareness of the importance of early recognition and treatment of a problem in arithmetic, willingness to take part in review sessions, and preference for addition over subtraction.

2.0 Responding: This category goes beyond the mere intention of doing something; it involves some action. This level also has three parts:

2.1 Acquiescence in Responding
2.2 Willingness to Respond
2.3 Satisfaction in Response

In Acquiescence in Responding (2.1), the desired behavior is described as compliance to teacher demands. Objectives at this level are directed at safety rules or discipline. The Willingness to Respond level (2.2) involves voluntary action on the part of the student. The next level (2.3) implies a satisfaction on the learner's part.

Suggested objectives for the 2.0 categories include the completion of mathematics homework, voluntary reading about modular arithmetic, and a broad smile from the student upon solving a linear equation.

3.0 Valuing: This category involves the idea that mathematics has worth and that learning mathematics is a worthwhile endeavor. There are three parts to the valuing category:

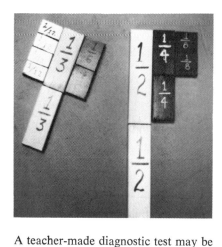

A teacher-made diagnostic test may be comprised of tasks at the concrete level as well as paper-pencil.

Children of the same age have different academic expectancies.

Since attitudes and emotions are directly involved in learning, a diagnostic strategy of teaching must include investigating a child's effective needs.

lassifying objects to form sets is a onceptual task represented concretely d underlies the notion of cardinality.

89

3.1 Acceptance of a Value
3.2 Preference of a Value
3.3 Commitment

Acceptance of a Value (3.1) involves exhibiting behavior that shows a belief in the worth of the activity. Behavior at the Preference for a Value level (3.2) is a bridge between 3.1 and 3.3. It involves more than just accepting a value, but less than commitment. Commitment (3.3) involves loyalty and certainty. At this level, the student is motivated by an underlying tension which needs to be satisfied.

Suggested objectives are continued conversation about mathematics concept by the student with friends outside of classroom situation; active participation in arranging a math and science fair; and indication of a long-term value for mathematics by the student.

4.0 Organization: Since some learning involves more than one value, it is necessary to organize values into a system, identify the relations between values, and notice the more powerful and lasting values. The two subsets of organization are:

4.1 Conceptualization of a Value
4.2 Organization of a Value System

The Conceptualization of a Value category (4.1) permits the student to see how the new value fits into his value system. The Organization of a Value System (4.2) consists of ordering one's concepts and makes allowances for the emergence of new values.

Suggested objectives here are the student's identification of the characteristics of a mathematical activity which he admires, and the student's development of a plan for regulating math "homework time" with "play time."

5.0 Characterization: At this level, the values are already in a hierarchy that has determined behavior. The two components of characterization are:

5.1 Generalized Set
5.2 Characterization

The Generalized Set level (5.1) may be considered a predictor or source of determination of the student's behavior. The Characterization category (5.2) defines the individual's philosophy of life. For example, the commitment to high academic achievement is shown by high level of performance in all academic areas.

Suggested objectives here are revision of the student's judgment in the light of new facts, and demonstration of consistently high achievement behavior in all areas.

An Instrument for Tapping Attitudes

Now that you have a structure for diagnosing in the affective domain, you will need a simple instrument for measuring attitudes toward mathematics. Charles Osgood's semantic differential technique is a helpful tool (Osgood, Suci, Tannenbaum, 1967) for use in tapping attitudes. It is made up of a list of bipolar adjectives weighted on a seven-point scale. An example follows:

Addition

1.	UGLY	BEAUTIFUL
2.	CHANGELESS	CHANGING
3.	WINDY	CALM
4.	STRANGE	FAMILIAR
5.	UNEXPLORED	EXPLORED
6.	UNPLEASANT	PLEASANT
7.	BAD	GOOD
8.	DIRTY	CLEAN
9.	HARMFUL	HELPFUL
10.	WORTHLESS	VALUABLE

The scale may be weighted in the following manner: -3 -2 -1 0 $+1$ $+2$ $+3$. Write the name of the concept to be tapped at the top of the set of scales. Add the plus scores and subtract the sum of the minus scores for each concept tapped. Then find the mean score. A positive score indicates a positive attitude.

Some other examples of concepts that might be measured in this way are subtraction, division, multiplication, sets, geometry, mathematics teacher, school, I-as-a-student, I-as-a-person.

Let us review the reactions of a student to the concept "I-as-a-person" and see how the attitude measure is derived.

I-as-a-Person

1.	UGLY	x		BEAUTIFUL
2.	CHANGELESS		x	CHANGING
3.	WINDY	x		CALM
4.	STRANGE		x	FAMILIAR
5.	UNEXPLORED	x		EXPLORED
6.	UNPLEASANT		x	PLEASANT
7.	BAD		x	GOOD
8.	DIRTY		x	CLEAN
9.	HARMFUL		x	HELPFUL
10.	WORTHLESS		x	VALUABLE

The numerical weightings for each bipolar pair are:*

1. -1	2. 0	4. $+1$
3. -1	6. 0	
5. -1	7. 0	
	8. 0	
	9. 0	
	10. 0	

* $-3 +0 +1 = -2$. Then divide this sum of -2 by ten (the number of bipolar pairs). Thus the score is $-.2$ for this concept.

A mean score of $-.2$ is obtained as the profile weighting for this child on the concept, "I-as-a-person." If other concepts show up negatively as well, you should apply Maslow's hierarchy of needs and Krathwohl, Bloom, and Masia's Affective Domain Taxonomy rather than emphasizing only the cognitive domain.

This is an oversimplified modification of Osgood's semantic differential. However, for the classroom teacher's use, a comparison of many children's scores on this task with their mathematics performance will prove helpful in identifying attitudes of children to arithmetic topics.

Concept of the
Integrated Person*

Carl Rogers (1959) has suggested that the client-centered psychotherapeutic situation may be compared to the student-teacher relation. Signifi-

---

* This section is based on "Significant Learning: In Therapy and in Education." *Educational Leadership* 16 (January 1959): 4, by permission of Robert R. Leeper, editor.

cant learning occurs in the psychotherapeutic relationship in much the same way as in the student-teacher relationship. This learning is more than a mere accumulation of facts. It makes a difference in the individual's behavior. The course of action he chooses in the future also is affected, as well as his attitude system and his personality.

Rogers presents five conditions of learning in psychotherapy. They are:

1. Facing A Problem;
2. Congruence;
3. Unconditional Positive Regard;
4. Empathetic Understanding; and
5. Perception of Therapist's Congruence.

These are described below and applied to an educational setting.

Facing A Problem

The individual is faced with a problem which he has tried—unsuccessfully —to cope with. He is eager to learn how to handle the problem but, at the same time, may be frightened that what he discovers in himself may be disturbing. Thus, one condition of learning is an uncertain and ambivalent desire, growing out of a perceived difficulty, to learn or to change.

The student who has met a challenge in mathematics performance is experiencing this uncertain and ambivalent desire to learn, but also may be frightened that the cause is unpleasant to him. He may be anxious to determine why he cannot divide decimal fractions, while at the same time, he may be resistant to help because he believes he is dumb.

I would take the comparison of the client-therapist relationship a step beyond the student-teacher situation. I believe further comparisons may be made regarding teacher-principal, teacher-supervisor, and principal-superintendent interactions. The teacher whose children have shown up consistently low in mathematics achievement may well encounter ambivalence in his or her desire to identify reasons for the poor performance of the class. Refresher courses in mathematics content or in how children learn elementary school mathematics may be needed. Is the teacher working at a concrete level when necessary or is it too much trouble to get out the manipulative materials? Is he or she able to identify the cause of a student's low performance as resulting from instruction or is it always the student's fault?

The principal whose entire school is performing poorly on mathematics achievement tests is facing a problem with his or her superintendent. Does he place the blame on his student population, on his teachers, on the atmosphere which he has created in his school building, or is he able to identify that the tests are not appropriate to the mathematics curriculum of his school? Is the principal able to seek help from his superiors or his colleagues? Is he able to face the problem, or is he even sure that it is a problem?

Congruence

Just as the therapist must be fully aware of what he is experiencing in the client-therapist relationship, so too must the teacher be aware of his own experiences. He must be accepting of his immediate feelings and make others feel comfortable and secure with him. We know exactly where he stands, for the integrated person says what he means and acts out what he believes. If he has had an unpleasant morning, he is aware of his feelings so that his students do not become the brunt of his internal disorder. This quality of congruence is essential in any human interaction—school, clinic, and the world in general.

Unconditional Positive Regard

This quality is best exemplified by the expression "I care." Involved is a safety-creating climate and the acceptance of both positive and negative expressions. The student who knows he can fail and still be accepted by those he loves and respects will not feel that he must buy love with high achievement. When the child knows that he will not be rejected or punished for poor achievement, he will not feel the need to cheat on evaluations. This is a very important quality in the diagnostic teacher. The "I care" attitude comes across to the student, who then begins to care about himself.

Empathetic Understanding

This level involves sensing the client's (or student's) world as if it were your own, without ever losing the "as if" quality. You sense the student's anger, fear, or confusion *as if* it were your own yet do not allow your own anger, fear or confusion to get bound up in it. It is then that you can help make your student aware of his feelings and guide him to understand them.

Often a student will become angry and not try to work out a mathematics problem. If you can empathize with his feelings without allowing yourself to become angry, you can better help to bring about a positive behavior in the student.

Perception of Therapist's Congruence

As the client must perceive and experience the therapist's congruence, acceptance, and empathy, so must the student. These conditions in the teacher must be communicated to the student.

When these five conditions exist, a process of change occurs. The students' rigid perception of himself and others loosens and becomes open to reality. Rogers (1959) has said that motivation doesn't come from the therapist (teacher) or the client (student), but, rather, "motivation for learning and change springs from the self-actualizing tendency of life itself, the tendency for the organism to flow into all the differentiated channels of potential development, insofar as these are experienced as enhancing."

Implications for Education

There are several implications for education imbedded in Carl Rogers' ideas. He seems to suggest "permitting the student at any level to be in real contact with the relevant problems of his existence so that he perceives those problems and issues which he wishes to resolve." The teacher's role, then, is to create a facilitating classroom climate in which real learning takes place. Then the teacher becomes a real person, not a "faceless embodiment of a curriculum requirement, or a sterile pipe through which knowledge is passed from one generation to the next."

The teacher must be aware that such accepting and empathetic behavior may free the student to express attitudes about parents, hatred of siblings, and feelings of concern about himself as he meets new situations and new material. Do such feelings have a right to exist openly in a school setting? Rogers says, "Yes. They are related to a person's becoming, to his effective learning and functioning."

Dealing with these feelings has a definite relationship to learning mathematics—or any other learning. Let us hypothesize that there are five natural tendencies in students:

1. Students in contact with life problems wish to learn.
2. They want to grow.
3. They seek to find out.
4. They hope to master.
5. They desire to create.

Therefore, the teacher must develop very personal relationships with his students and create a classroom climate which allows these five natural tendencies to evolve and mature.

10

Guidelines for Preparing a Teacher-Made Diagnostic Test

Following is a sequence of steps for building a teacher-made diagnostic test.

I. Select Content for Diagnostic Test.

List the areas of weakness for the class (or individual) that were identified on survey tests. (Survey test may be achievement tests in arithmetic, standardized diagnostic tests, end-of-the-chapter book tests, grade level tests, exercises in the arithmetic text, or teacher–made surveys.)

II. Isolate one concept that is to be diagnosed indepth.

Apply Gagne's idea of necessary prerequisites and learning sequences to analyze the components which make up the particular concept. Arrange these subconcepts in a logical teaching sequence so that prerequisite skills or concepts precede those behaviors that depend on them (see page 33).

III. Determine at what level of learning the individual is (or at what level the majority of students are performing).

A. Use Brownell's or Gagne's hierarchies, described on pages 60–75 of this book.
B. Administer Piaget's number conservation tasks, described on pages 55–59, to determine if the student has such mathematical

ideas as one-to-one correspondence, reversibility, identity, or seriation. These are basic to elementary school mathematics.
C. Apply Maslow's hierarchy of needs (see pages 83–87) to determine whether the student's learning difficulties may stem from emotional or social needs rather than from intellectual causes.
   1. Observe the child in many school situations (classroom, playground, gym, lunch, free time).
   2. Make a home visit, if possible, to meet the child's family.
D. Decide where the student fits in Krathwohl, Bloom and Masia's Affective Domain taxonomy.

VI. Decide on the behaviors you want the child to display in order to show that he has acquired the particular concept.

   Apply Bloom, Engelhart, Furst, Hill and Krathwohl's Cognitive Domain Taxonomy as described on pages 75–77 of this book.

V. Write a table of specification which includes the behavior and content components to serve as the structure for your diagnostic test. An example of a table of specification may be found in the following section of this book and will serve as a guide through building a diagnostic test.

VI. Build the test, asking the following questions:

A. Is it all paper-pencil?
B. Will you need to include activities with concrete objects?
C. Will the testing situation parallel the teaching situation so that test items are a true reflection of the instruction?
D. Will you include extrapolation activities to show transfer of present knowledge to new situations?
E. Will you include items that require pointing responses for children who have difficulty producing a written response?

VII. Interview the student (or class members) in regard to items missed in order to determine the validity of the item. Is the item really measuring what you think it is, or has the child missed it because of a misinterpretation of what is being asked?

Guiding You through
Building a Diagnostic Test

The following activities provide a series of mini-tests, each built on a single concept or skill. If you build a file of single-concept diagnostic tests, you can combine appropriate mini-tests into a broader diagnosis depending on the identified content needs.

Content 1: Equivalent Sets

Desired Behavior:　　　To recognize equivalent sets.

Prerequisite Behavior:
1. To recognize objects.
2. To name objects.
3. To match like objects.
4. To name like objects.
5. To identify like objects.
6. To pair like objects.
7. To pair unlike objects.
8. To match two sets of like objects in a one-to-one correspondence.
9. To select equivalent sets.
10. Perform behaviors 1 to 9 at the picture level.
11. Perform behaviors 1 to 9 at the symbolic level.

Table of Specification:

Equivalent Sets	Behaviors				
	A. To indicate	B. To name	C. To match	D. To identify	E. To pair
1. Sets of objects.					
2. Pictures of sets.					
3. Sets of numerals or words.					

Suggestions for diagnostic test items are keyed to the content and behavior as shown on the Table of Specification on page 99:

1A. Show child five red straws, five red blocks, and three yellow blocks. Say, "Point to set of red blocks."

1B. For each set say, "Tell me what these are" (use objects in 1A).

1C. Say, "Match the sets having red objects" (use objects in 1A).

1D. Say, "Show me the set of three" (use objects in 1A).

1E. Say, "Match the two sets having the same number of objects."

2A. Show child drawing or pictures of objects. Say, "Point to picture of red blocks."

2B–2E. Use the same procedure as that for "Sets of objects" but use pictures.

3A–3E. Use the same procedures as 1A–1E. but use numerals or words in place of objects.

Content 2: Relations between Whole Numbers

Table of Specification:

	Behavior				
Whole Numbers	A. To count	B. To enumerate	C. To assign	D. To represent order	E. To identify
1. Numbers					
2. Sets					
3. Numeral					

Desired Behavior: To identify the larger (or smaller) of two numbers.

Prerequisite Behavior: 1. To count numbers aloud.

2. To enumerate objects.

3. To place sets in order of size from smallest to largest.

4. To assign a number to a set of objects.

5. To represent the ascending order of sets with numerals.

6. To identify the numeral representing the larger of two numbers.

Suggestions for diagnostic test items:

1A. Ask child to count aloud as far as he can.

1B. Ask child to enumerate objects in a set [Note the difference between counting and enumerating. Counting involves verbal associations (Gagne's Type 4 learning)]. Basic to enumerating is the notion of one-to-one correspondence. See page 55 of this book.

1C. Show sets of objects. Ask the child to tell you how many objects are in a set.

1D. Place sets in order, smallest to largest. Tell the child to write numerals to represent the order of these sets.

2B. Show child sets of objects. Say, "Count the objects in this set." Continue with other sets.

2C. Say, "Write the numeral that shows how many objects are in the set."

3C. Same as 2C.

3D. Show sets having cardinal number properties of 1 to 9. Say same as for 2C.

3E. Show "7 to 9." Say, "Draw a circle around the numeral representing the larger number."

Content 3: Place Value

Desired Behavior: To write numbers named by two digits.
Prerequisite Behavior: 1. To select equivalent sets

2. To identify the larger (or smaller) of two numbers
3. To add whole numbers
4. To multiply whole numbers

Table of Specification:

Place Value	Behavior						
	A. To select	B. To identify	C. To group	D. To name	E. To show	F. To count	write G. To
1. Equivalent sets	✓						
2. Unequal numbers		✓					
3. Concrete objects			✓				
4. Number names				✓			
5. Number of groups				✓			
6. Objects in many-to-one relation					✓		
7. From 1 to 9 objects						✓	
8. Place values			✓				
9. Using place value						✓	
10. Abacus representation of 2-digit numeral					✓		✓

Table of Specification (cont.)

Place Value	Behavior						
	A. To select	B. To identify	C. To group	D. To name	E. To show	F. To count	G. To write
11. Picture representation of 2-digit numeral							✓
12. 2-digit numerals				✓			
13. Face value and place value of a digit in a numeral				✓			

Suggestions for diagnostic test items:

3C. Ask the child to bundle a collection of sticks into groups of ten with from zero to nine extra single sticks.

4D. Ask the child to read aloud number names from zero to nine. Then following concrete level activities that emerge from prerequisite behavior 9–13, extend reading aloud numerals beyond nine.

6E. Ask the student to show that a bundle of ten sticks may be represented by an agreed upon single object.

7F. Instruct the student to count from one to nine beads on a 9-bead abacus.

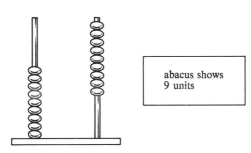

abacus shows
9 units

8D. Ask the child to name the place values of an abacus.

9F. Have the student count to ten on a 9-bead abacus by applying place value.

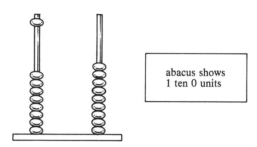

abacus shows
1 ten 0 units

10E. Say a number greater than nine and ask the child to show this number on the abacus.

10G. Show a 2-digit number on the abacus and tell the child to write the number shown.

11G. Ask the child to write 2-digit numerals from picture representations.

12D. Ask the child to write the numerals from 19 through 30. (This activity may be extended from 10 to 99)

12G. Ask the child to read aloud the numerals from 19 through 30. (Extend from 10 to 99)

13D. Ask the child to state the face value and place value of a digit in a numeral.

Extension of 12D. Ask child to read aloud:

| 45 | 378 | 9867 | 303 |

Extension of 12B. Ask the child to write an X on the correct numeral as you read aloud from the following table:

7	7831	1500	436
403	6	909	90
391	43	330	8

Extension of 12G. Dictate the following for the child to write as a numeral:

1. thirty-five   2. one hundred three

3. nine thousand four hundred twenty

Content 4: Addition of Whole Numbers with Renaming

Desired Behavior: To add, with renaming, a one digit number to a two digit number.

Prerequisite Behavior: 1. To compute correctly the basic addition combinations.
2. To write a numeral correctly by employing place value.
3. To rename ten ones as one ten.
4. To compute using addition algorithm.

Table of Specification:

Addition with Renaming	Behavior		
	A. To compute	B. To write	C. To rename
1. Basic addition combinations			
2. Numeral			
3. Ones and Tens			
4. Addition Algorithm			

Suggestions for diagnostic test items:

1A. Ask the child to compute the basic addition combinations by completing the addition grid:

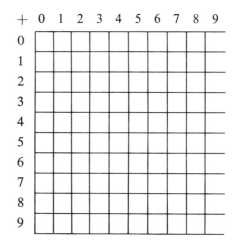

2B. Ask child to complete the following in the form:

$$3 \text{ ones, } 2 \text{ tens} = \underline{23}$$

1. 7 ones, 4 tens = _____
2. 3 hundreds, 5 tens, 2 ones = _____
3. 4 thousands, 2 tens = _____
4. 2 ones, 3 tens, 9 hundreds = _____

2C. Ask child to complete:

1. thirteen ones = _____ tens, _____ ones
2. twenty-three ones = _____ tens, _____ ones
3. one hundred thirty = _____ tens
4. 347 = 2 hundreds, _____ tens, 7 ones

3C. Complete the following:

1. 3 tens and 4 ones = 2 tens and _____ ones
2. 17 ones and 9 tens = _____ tens and 7 ones
3. 2 tens and 75 ones = _____ tens and 5 ones
4. 9 tens and 83 ones = _____ hundreds, _____ tens, 3 ones

4A. Compute:

1.	18	2.	75	3.	92	4.	84
	+9		+5		+8		+9

11

Reisman Sequential Assessment Mathematics Inventory (SAMI)*

The Sequential Assessment Mathematics Inventory (SAMI) presented here is comprised of four parts: Part 1 for grades kindergarten, one, and two; Part 2 for grades three and four; Part 3 for grades five and six; and Part 4 for grades seven and eight. SAMI is also appropriate at higher grade levels for older students who lack basic mathematics knowledge. It may be necessary in some cases to administer a lower level part of SAMI to those students who cannot perform successfully on even the initial items comprising the part of the assessment that is equivalent to their grade in school (see discussion on underachiever, page 49).

All items on this diagnostic tool are keyed to eighteen mathematics ideas. This is to help you quickly identify those areas which are problematic to a student or group of students. Also presented are selected answers to items on SAMI. Once the areas of weakness have been identified, specific performance objectives for instruction may be developed. The areas of strength aid in selecting instructional procedures that have proven effective with the particular student(s). In addition to analyzing results of SAMI, it must be remembered that day-to-day observations are important. The student's emotional aspects must be considered as well as his or her cognitive activities.

The performance objectives were used as the structure for diagnostic items on SAMI. These items may also be used as instructional activities forming the instructional component of the Diagnostic Teaching Cycle (see page 7).

---

* Copyright 1977 by Fredricka K. Reisman.

107

The SAMI items are categorized as to type of learning and mode of representing curriculum or content for each item (see page 132). Preceding this categorization is the Table of Specification that underlies the Sequential Assessment Mathematics Inventory, Parts 1, 2, 3, and 4. Individual and Class Profiles are presented following the type of learning summary (see pages 134–143 for profile formats).

**Performance Objectives
Underlying the SAMI**

Part 1: Grades K, 1, and 2

Content   *Performance Objective*

1. Proximity
   a. To place an object close to a given object.
   b. To draw a figure close to a given figure.

2. Spatial Relations
   a. To complete a puzzle.
   b. To move an object upwards in space (down).
   c. To place an object under (over) a given object.
   d. To place an object within a given enclosure.
   e. To place objects in an indicated order.
   f. To place an object between two given objects.

3. Size
   a. To select the larger (smaller) of two objects.
   b. To arrange objects from shortest to longest.

4. Numeration
   a. To write the digits 0 to 9.
   b. To indicate the cardinal number property of a set by selecting the appropriate flannel board numerals.
   c. To write the numeral which represents the cardinality of a set.

5. Cardinality
   a. To match objects in sets showing one-to-one correspondence.
   b. To enumerate objects in a set.

Content	*Performance Objective*
6. Classification	a. To describe what is alike about two or more objects (or sets).
	b. To arrange objects into groups so all objects within a group are alike in some way.
7. Equivalent Sets	a. To label equivalent sets with the numeral that indicates their equivalence.
	b. To draw a set that is equivalent to a given set.
	c. To use the $=$ symbol when appropriate.
8. Nonequivalence	a. To select the nonequivalent set from a group of sets.
	b. To draw a set that has a greater number of objects than a given set.
	c. To use correctly the inequality symbols $(<, >)$.
9. Addition	a. To record an addition example shown on a number line.
	b. To record an addition example shown by unionizing sets.
	c. To show the commutative property with sets, pictures, and/or addition equations.
	d. To show the associative property with sets, pictures, and/or equations.
	e. To show the additive identity with sets, pictures, and/or equations.
	f. To add on an abacus.
	g. To compute without renaming.
10. Multiplication	a. To show union of disjoint equivalent sets as a model for simple multiplication examples.
	b. To record simple multiplication examples shown with sets and/or pictures.
	c. To relate the place value idea to multiplication.
11. Place Value	a. To show ten units as one ten.
	b. To show ten tens as one hundred.

Content	*Performance Objective*
	c. To describe why $9 + 1$ may not be expressed as a 1-digit numeral in base ten.
	d. To compare our place value notational system with an ancient nonpositional system.
	e. To relate multiplication to generating place values.
	f. To enumerate beads on a nine bead abacus showing that the $9 + 1$ sum is shown by a move to the tens position.
	g. To employ place value in addition and multiplication computations when recording the vertical algorithms.
12. Subtraction	a. To employ place value in subtraction when recording the vertical algorithm.
	b. To record simple subtraction examples shown with sets and/or pictures (no renaming).

Part 2: Grades 3 and 4*

Prerequisite: Ability to perform Part 1 of SAMI.

Content	*Performance Objective*
12. Subtraction	c. To show subtraction as the inverse relation to addition.
	d. To record the subtraction problem for simple verbal problems (no renaming).
	e. To complete an addition-subtraction grid.
	f. To subtract on a nine bead abacus (no renaming).
	g. To relate renaming one ten as ten units to the addition operation where ten units are renamed as one ten.
	h. To subtract with renaming.
9. Addition of Whole Numbers	h. To add with renaming using sets, pictures, and/or algorithms.

* Note: Part 2, Grades 3 and 4, also includes Objectives 6 through 12b.

Content	*Performance Objective*
	i. To record the addition problem for related verbal problems, with and without renaming.
10. Multiplication	d. Write multiplication equations that describe sets and/or pictures.
	e. Record multiplication equations shown on number lines.
	f. Write the factors for a number.
	g. To show the Distributive Property of Multiplication over Addition with sets, pictures, and/or equations.
13. Division	a. To show division on a number line.
	b. To show uneven and even division with dot arrays.
	c. To relate division as the inverse operation of multiplication.
	d. To show division as repeated subtraction of the same number.
	e. To compute simple division problems.
14. Prime Numbers	a. To write prime numbers.
	b. To discriminate prime from composite numbers.
	c. To write a composite number as a product of its primes.
10. Multiplication of Whole Numbers	h. Write the lowest common multiple (LCM) of two or more numbers.
	i. Write the greatest common factor (GCF) of two or more numbers.
15. Fractions	a. To divide a figure into a designated number of parts.
	b. To write the number of fractional parts into which a whole has been divided.
	c. Write the appropriate numerator to show how many parts of the whole figure is being considered.
	d. Write the appropriate numerator and denominator for a group of objects (either real or pictured).
	e. Write equivalent fraction names for the number one.

Content	*Performance Objective*
	f. Show fractions on a number line.
	g. Write equivalent fractions from concrete, and/or picture representations.
	h. Write equivalent fractions for a given fraction.
	i. Perform simple multiplication of fractions.

Part 3: Grades 5 and 6*

Prerequisite: Ability to perform Part 2 of SAMI.

Content	*Performance Objective*
10. Multiplication of Whole Numbers	j. To complete a multiplication grid.
15. Fractions	j. To multiply mixed fractions.
	k. To divide fractions.
	l. To add fractions with like and unlike denominators.
	m. To subtract fractions with like and unlike denominators.

Content	*Performance Objective*
16. Decimals	a. Divide units by ten to obtain decimal fractions.
	b. To add and subtract decimals with and without renaming.
	c. To multiply decimals.
	d. To divide decimals.
	e. To convert fractions to their equivalent decimal form.
	f. To convert decimals to their equivalent fraction form.
	g. To relate percent to decimal fractions.
	h. To solve percent problems.
17. Geometry	a. Find the supplement and complement of angles.
	b. Graph designated points on an x,y axis.
	c. Use metric measures.
	d. Find the perimeter of a given figure.

---

* Note: Part 3, Grades 5 and 6, also includes Objectives 9c through 15i.

Part 4: Grades 7 and 8*

Prerequisites: Ability to perform Part 3 of SAMI.

Content	*Performance Objective*
17. Geometry	e. To find the volume of a given figure.
	f. To find the diameter of a circle when the radius is given.
	g. To find the circumference of a circle when the radius is given.
	h. To find the area of a given figure.
	i. To draw a simple closed curve.
	j. To show translations and rotations.
	k. To identify figures that have line symmetry.
18. Probability and Statistics	a. To write as a fraction the probability of a given event to occur.
	b. To interpret bar graphs.
	c. To interpret descriptive statistics.

Directions for Administering SAMI

Read instructions to the student when necessary unless the item is testing reading comprehension, as in verbal problem solving. For young children or for those who have had little success in mathematics, you may wish to copy the test items on index cards and administer only one item at a time. This procedure will help to eliminate the possibility of the child's becoming overwhelmed at the sight of a long-looking test. Proceed from the lowest level of learning to the highest so that the student will experience success as he works his way up to the higher levels of learning.

Scoring of SAMI

In scoring items on the Sequential Assessment Mathematics Inventory, an item is counted correctly only if all of its components are answered correctly. This helps to compensate for a child obtaining parts of an item correct by chance or by guessing.

---

* Note: Part 4, Grades 7 and 8, also includes Objectives 13a through 17d.

If the student answers 80 percent of the questions in one part of the Inventory correctly, go on to the next part. If the student does not reach the 80 percent criterion, go back to the next lower grade level test (that is, go from Part 2 to Part 1) in order to identify the level at which he or she is performing.

SAMI Part 1: Grades K–2

4a. Fill in the missing numbers. 0 __ __ 3 __ 5 __ __ __ 9	7c. Write the equal sign where needed.
4c. Write the number to show that four objects are in the set. 	8a. Mark X on the set that is different in number.
7a. Write the correct number that shows how many are in each set. 	8b. Draw a set that is greater in number than this set.
7b. Draw the same number of circles in Set B as are in Set A. Set A Set B	8c. Fill in the correct sign to make a true sentence. 6 ____ 9 4 ____ 2 3 ____ 5 8 ____ 9

9a. Show that $2 + 3 = 5$ on the number line.

9g. Add the following.

$$\begin{array}{ccc} 41 & 24 & 17 \\ +23 & +13 & +62 \\ \hline \end{array}$$

9b. How many objects are there altogether?

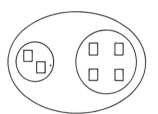

_____

10a. Using the bags of candy, fill in the numbers below to tell how many pieces of candy there are.

___ + ___ + ___ = 6

3 twos = 6

3 × ___ = ___

9c. Complete the following to make the sentences true.

$2 + 3 =$ _____ $+2$

$\square + \boxplus = \boxplus +$ ___

10b. Write the multiplication sentence for this picture.

○ ○ ○   ○ ○ ○   ○ ○ ○   ○ ○ ○

_____

9d. Complete the following to make the sentences true.

$(2 + 3) + 4 = 2 +(3 +$ ___ $)$

$(\_+ 6) + 7 = 8 +(\_+ 7)$

10c. Complete the following place value chart.

thousands _____ tens   units

_____ × _____ × _____ × _____

9e. Complete the following.

$3 +$ __ $= 3$

11a. Show how many tens by circling groups of ten.

□□□□□□□□□

115

11b. What number is ten groups of ten?
Write the number in the box below.

\#\#\#\#\#\#\#\#\#\#   @@@@@@@@@@

¢¢¢¢¢¢¢¢¢   ★★★★★★★★★★

%%%%%%%%% $$$$$$$$$$

☐☐☐☐☐☐☐☐☐   &&&&&&&&&&

%%%%%%%%%   ☐☐☐☐☐☐☐☐☐☐

11f. Mark the abacus that shows $9 + 1$.

tens ones   tens ones   tens ones   tens ones

11g. Complete the following.

$$\begin{array}{r} 32 \\ \times 24 \\ \hline \end{array} \qquad \begin{array}{r} 36 \\ \times 23 \\ \hline \end{array}$$

12a. The problem $65 - 23 = \square$ can be written as

$$\begin{array}{r} 65 \\ -23 \\ \hline 42. \end{array}$$

In the box below, write the following problem this way and find the answer.

$$47 - 32 = \square$$

12b. Write a subtraction sentence to tell about the picture.

⊗⊗⊗⊗○○

Note: Part 1, Grades K–2, should also include items based upon performance Objectives 1 through 3b, which are at the concrete level rather than paper-pencil.

116

12c. Complete the following. $4 + 7 =$ _____ _____ $- 7 = 4$ _____ $- 4 = 7$	**9h.** Complete the following. $\quad\quad 37 \quad\quad\quad 59$ $\quad\quad +26 \quad\quad +74$
12d. Mark the sentence that solves the problem. Sam has 5 marbles. Jan takes 3 marbles away. How many marbles does Sam have left? $5 + 3 = 8 \quad\quad 5 - 3 = 2 \quad\quad 3 + 2 = 5$	**9i.** Larry had 13 rocks in a sack. On his way home from school, he picked up 9 more rocks. How many rocks does he now have? _____
12e. Complete the grid.	**10d.** Write the multiplication sentence for the picture.  _____

12e. grid:

+/−	6	3	2
8	14		10
4	10	7	
		12	11

12h. Complete the following. $\quad 62 \quad\quad 35$ $\quad -48 \quad -19$	**10e.** Show that $3 \times 3 = 9$ on the number line. $\quad 0 \; 1 \; 2 \; 3 \; 4 \; 5 \; 6 \; 7 \; 8 \; 9 \; 10 \; 11 \; 12$

117

10f. List factors for 18, greater than 1.

$18 = \underline{\quad} \times \underline{\quad}$

$18 = \underline{\quad} \times \underline{\quad} \times \underline{\quad}$

10g. Mark X on the correct number sentences.

$5\,(3 + 6) = 5\,(3) + 5\,(6)$

$5 + (3 \times 6) = (5 + 3) \times (5 \times 6)$

$5\,(3 \times 6) = 5\,(3) \times 5\,(6)$

$\square\,(* + @) = \square* + \square@$

13a. Show on a number line the number sentence $8 \div 2 = 4$.

0 1 2 3 4 5 6 7 8

13b. Group the array to show $17 \div 2 = \underline{\quad}$

13c. Complete the following number sentences.

$18 \div 3 = \underline{\quad}$

$\underline{\quad} \times 3 = 18$

13d. Show on a number line $15 \div 5 = \underline{\quad\quad}$.

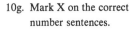

13e. Complete the following.

$8 \div 2 = \underline{\quad}$

$6 \div 3 = \underline{\quad}$ $3\overline{)15}$

14a. Write the prime numbers between 1 and 25.

$\underline{\quad}\ \ \underline{\quad}\ \ \underline{\quad}\ \ \underline{\quad}\ \ \underline{\quad}$

$\underline{\quad}\ \ \underline{\quad}\ \ \underline{\quad}\ \ \underline{\quad}$

14b. Circle the prime numbers.

    1   6   2   8   11   18   22

14c. Write 24 as a product of primes.

$$24 = \underline{\quad} \times \underline{\quad} \times \underline{\quad} \times \underline{\quad}$$

10h. Write the lowest common multiple (LCM) of 8 and 6.

       _____

10i. Write the greatest common factor (GCF) for 36 and 24.

       _____

15a. Divide the figure into 4 equal size parts.

15b. Write the number to show how many parts the figure has been divided into.

15c. Write the numerator to show how many parts are shaded.

   ____

15d. Write a fraction to name the shaded part of the group below.

   ____

15e. Write 3 fraction names for the number 1.

  _____   _____   _____

119

15f. Show the fraction 5/6 on the number line below.

0   1

Note: Part 2, Grades 3–4, should also include items based upon performance Objectives 6 through 12b.

15g. Show on a number line that $1/2 = 2/4$.

0   1

15h. Write three equivalent fraction names for $1/2$.

$$\frac{1}{2} = \underline{\hspace{1cm}} = \underline{\hspace{1cm}} = \underline{\hspace{1cm}}$$

15i. Complete the following.

$2/3 \times 4/5 =$

$7/8 \times 5/6 =$

120

10j. Complete the following multiplication grid.

×	5	7	3
4	20		12
8			
6			

15j. Complete the following.

$5\frac{1}{4}$
$\times 3$
$\qquad$ $3\frac{1}{2} \times 2\frac{1}{4} =$

15k. Complete the following.

$$\frac{7}{12} \div \frac{3}{4} =$$

$$\frac{35}{27} \div \frac{7}{3} =$$

15l. Complete the following.

$\frac{3}{4}$
$\frac{2}{+\,4}$ $\qquad$ $\frac{7}{8}$
$\frac{2}{+\,3}$

15m. Complete the following.

$$\frac{3}{3} - \frac{1}{3} = \underline{\qquad}$$

$$\frac{6}{8} - \frac{1}{8} = \underline{\qquad}$$

16a. Write in decimal form.

$$2 \div 10 = \underline{\qquad}$$

$$7 \div 100 = \underline{\qquad}$$

16b. Complete the following.

2.44	3.74	4.74
+2.35	+1.29	− .35

16c. Complete the following.

.23	.43	7.3
× .2	×.12	×2.4

121

16d. Divide the following decimals.

$$.36 \div .6 = \underline{\hspace{2cm}}$$

$$.24 \div .8 = \underline{\hspace{2cm}}$$

$$.7\overline{)48.3}$$

16e. Write the following fractions as decimals.

$$3/6 = \underline{\hspace{1.5cm}} \qquad 5/10 = \underline{\hspace{1.5cm}}$$

$$3/4 = \underline{\hspace{1.5cm}} \qquad 2/3 = \underline{\hspace{1.5cm}}$$

16f. Write the decimals below as fractions.

$$.23 = \underline{\hspace{1.5cm}} \qquad .25 = \underline{\hspace{1.5cm}}$$

$$.3 = \underline{\hspace{1.5cm}}$$

16g. Write 75 % as a decimal.

$$75 \% = \underline{\hspace{2cm}}$$

16h. Write 30 % of 17.

$$30 \% \text{ of } 17 = \underline{\hspace{2cm}}$$

17a. Find the supplement of angle A.

$$A = 50°$$

$$\underline{\hspace{2cm}}$$

17b. Graph the following points on the x,y axis below. (3,4), (2,−2), (−1,3).

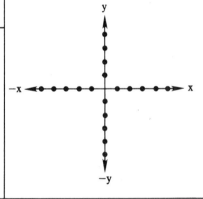

122

17c. Complete the following.

$$6 \text{ cm} = \underline{\hspace{2cm}} \text{ mm}$$

$$3 \text{ km} = \underline{\hspace{2cm}} \text{ m}$$

17d. Find the perimeter of the given rectangular region.

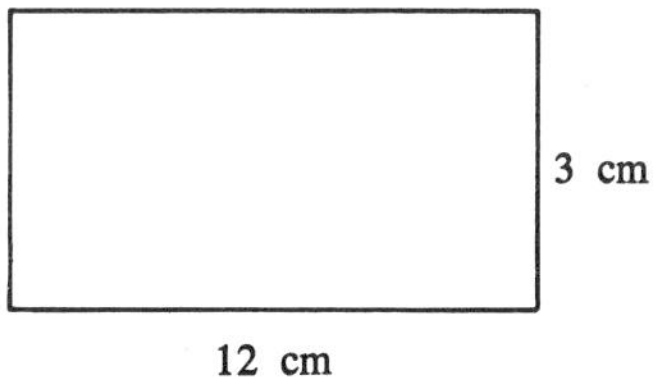

3 cm

12 cm

Note: Part 3, Grades 5–6, should also include items based upon performance Objectives 9c through 15i.

123

17e. Find the volume of the following figure.

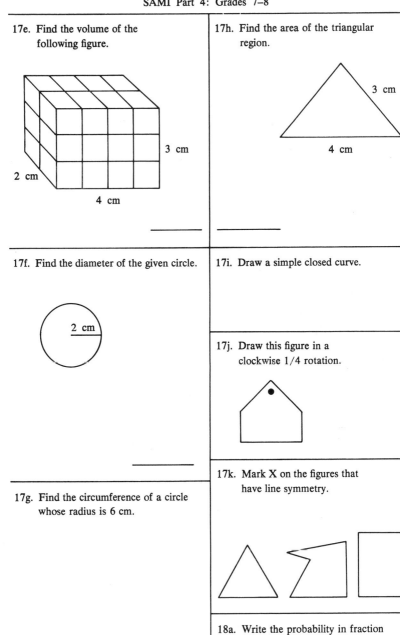

3 cm

2 cm

4 cm

17f. Find the diameter of the given circle.

2 cm

17g. Find the circumference of a circle whose radius is 6 cm.

17h. Find the area of the triangular region.

3 cm

4 cm

17i. Draw a simple closed curve.

17j. Draw this figure in a clockwise 1/4 rotation.

17k. Mark X on the figures that have line symmetry.

18a. Write the probability in fraction form for a coin tossed ten times to come up heads.

18b. On a visit to the zoo, Johnny saw bears, zebras, monkeys, and tigers. How many bears and how many tigers did he see as shown on the graph below?

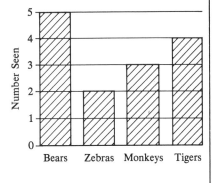

Bears _____   Tigers _____

Note: Part 4, Grades 7–8, should also include items based upon performance Objectives 13a through 17d.

18c. Following are test scores for 3 students, Ann, Barbara, and Catherine. Who has the highest mean score? What is this mean?

Ann's scores: 89, 72,80,56,98

Barbara's score: 72,93,56

Catherine's scores: 90,91,90,92,35

Student with highest mean is:

Mean = _____

125

Selected Answers to SAMI

Part 1: Grades K–2

7c.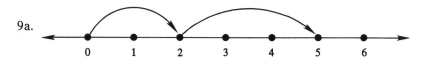

8c. $6 < 9, 3 < 5, 4 > 2, 8 < 9$

9a.

9b. 6

9c. $2 + 3 = 3 + 2,$ $\square + \boxplus = \boxplus + \square$

9d. $(2+3)+4=2+(3+4), (8+6)+7=8+(6+7)$

9e. $3+0=3$

10a. $2 + 2 + 2 = 6, 3 \times 2 = 6$

10b. $4 \times 3 = 12$

10c. hundreds, $10 \times 10 \times 10 \times 1$

11b. 100

11f.

12a. $\begin{array}{r} 47 \\ -32 \\ \hline 15 \end{array}$

12b. $6-4 = 2$ or $\begin{array}{r} 6 \\ -4 \\ \hline 2 \end{array}$

Part 2: Grades 3–4

12c. $4 + 7 = 11$ $11 - 7 = 4$ $11 - 4 = 7$

12d. $5 - 3 = 2$

12e. 14, *11*, 10
10, 7, *6*
9 15, 12, 11

12h. $\begin{array}{r} 62 \\ -48 \\ \hline 14 \end{array}$ $\begin{array}{r} 35 \\ -19 \\ \hline 16 \end{array}$

9h. $\begin{array}{r} 37 \\ +26 \\ \hline 63 \end{array}$ $\begin{array}{r} 59 \\ +74 \\ \hline 133 \end{array}$

9i. $\begin{array}{r} 13 \\ +9 \\ \hline 22 \end{array}$

10d. $3 \times 5 = 15$

10e.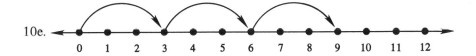

10f. $18 = 3 \times 6$ $18 = 2 \times 9$ $18 = 2 \times 3 \times 3$

10g. $5(3+6) = 5(3) + 5(6)$, $\square(* + @) = \square* + \square@$

13a.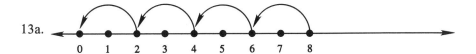

13c. $18 \div 3 = 6$ $6 \times 3 = 18$

14a. 2, 3, 5, 7, 11, 13, 17, 19, 23

14b. 2,11

14c. $24 = 2 \times 2 \times 2 \times 3$

10h. LCM = 24

10i. GCF = 12

15a. or

15c. 5

15d. 2/5

15e. 2/2, 3/3, 4/4, . . .

15f.

15g.
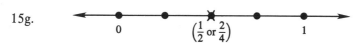

15h. $1/2 = 2/4 = 3/6 = 4/8, \ldots$

15i. 8/15, 35/48

Part 3: Grades 5–6

10j. 20, *28*, 12
40, *56*, 24
30, 42, 18

15j. $15\frac{3}{4}$, $3\frac{1}{2} \times 2\frac{1}{4} = \left(3 + \frac{1}{2}\right)\left(2 + \frac{1}{4}\right)$

$$= (3 \times 2) + \left(3 \times \frac{1}{4}\right) + \left(\frac{1}{2} \times 2\right) + \left(\frac{1}{2} \times \frac{1}{4}\right)$$

$$= \quad 6 \quad + \frac{3}{4} + \frac{2}{2} + \frac{1}{8}$$

$$= \quad 7 + \frac{3}{4} + \frac{1}{8}$$

$$= \quad 7 + \frac{6}{8} + \frac{1}{8}$$

$$= \quad 7 + \frac{7}{8}$$

$$= 7\frac{7}{8}$$

15k. $\frac{7}{12} \div \frac{3}{4} = \frac{7}{\cancel{12}_{3}} \times \frac{\cancel{4}^{1}}{3} = \frac{7}{9}$

$\frac{35}{27} \div \frac{7}{3} = \frac{5}{9}$

15l. $\frac{5}{4}, \; \frac{7}{8} + \frac{2}{3} = \frac{21}{24} + \frac{16}{24} = \frac{37}{24} = 1\frac{13}{24}$

15m. 2/3, 5/8

16a. .2, .07

16b. 4.79, 5.03, 4.39

16c. .046, .0516, 17.52

16d. .6, .3, 69

16e. .5, .75, .5, .6$\overline{6}$

16f. 23/100, 25/100 or 1/4, 3/10

16g. .75

16h. 5.1

17a. 130°

17b.

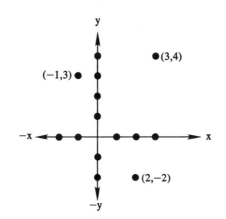

17c. 60mm, 3000m

17d. 36 cm²

Part 4: Grades 7–8

17e. 24 cm³

17f. d = 4 cm

17g. C = πd   d = 2r
           = π 12 cm or 12πcm

17h. A = 1/2 bh
           = 1/2 (12)
           = 6 cm²

17i.

17j.

17k.

18a. $1/2$ or $\dfrac{5}{10}$

18.b. bears—5, tigers—4

18c. Ann's mean equals 79; Barbara's mean $= 73.7$; Catherine's mean $= 79.6$; Catherine has the highest mean score.

Table of Specification

SAMI Part 1: Grades K–2

	Behavior			
Content	Show	Write	Interpret	Compute
Proximity	1a, 1b			
Spatial Relations	2a–2f			
Size	3a, 3b			
Numeration	4b, 7c	4a, 4c	7a	
Cardinality	5a, 5b			
Classification	6b		6a	
Equivalent sets	7b			
Nonequivalence	8a, 8b	8c		
Addition of whole numbers	9c, 9d, 9e	9a, 9b		9f, 9g
Multiplication of whole numbers	10a	10b	10c	
Place Value	11a, 11b, 11f		11c, 11d, 11e	11g
Subtraction of whole numbers			12b	12a

SAMI Part 2: Grades 3–4

	Behavior			
Content	Show	Analyze	Interpret	Compute
Subtraction of whole numbers	12f	12d	12c, 12g	12e, 12h
Addition of whole numbers	9h		9i	
Multiplication of whole numbers	10g	10f, 10h, 10i	10d, 10e	

Table of Specification (cont.)
SAMI Part 2: Grades 3–4

	Behavior			
Content	Show	Write	Interpret	Compute
Division of whole numbers	13a, 13b	13d	13c	13e
Prime Numbers		14a, 14c	14b	
Fractions	15a, 15f	15e, 15d, 15g, 15h	15b, 15c	15i

SAMI Part 3: Grades 5–6

	Behavior			
Content	Show	Interpret	Translate	Compute
Multiplication of whole numbers				10j
Fractions				15j–15m
Decimals		16g	16e, 16f	16a–16d, 16h
Geometry	17b			17a, 17c, 17d

SAMI Part 4: Grades 7–8

	Behavior			
Content	Show	Identify	Interpret	Compute
Geometry	17i, 17j	17k		17e–17h
Probability and Statistics			18b, 18c	18a

Type of Learning and Mode of Representation of Items Comprising the SAMI

Item	Type of Learning	Mode	Item	Type of Learning	Mode
Part 1					
4a	motor chaining	symbolic	7b	concept	iconic
4c	arbitrary association	symbolic	7c	principle	symbolic
			8a	principle	iconic
7a	concept	symbolic	8b	principle	iconic

Item	Type of Learning	Mode	Item	Type of Learning	Mode
8c	principle	symbolic	10i	principle	symbolic
9a	principle	iconic	15a	principle	iconic
9b	principle	iconic	15b	concept	iconic
9c	principle	symbolic	15c	principle	iconic
9d	principle	symbolic	15d	principle	iconic
9e	principle	symbolic	15e	principle	symbolic
9g	prob.solv.	symbolic	15f	concept	iconic
10a	principle	iconic-symbolic	15g	principle	iconic
			15h	principle	symbolic
10b	principle	iconic-symbolic	15i	principle	symbolic
10c	principle	symbolic	*Part 3*		
11a	concept	iconic			
11b	principle	iconic-symbolic	10j	principle	symbolic
			15j	prob.solv.	symbolic
11f	multiple discrimination	iconic	15k	principle	symbolic
			15l	principle	symbolic
11g	prob.solv.	symbolic	15m	principle	symbolic
12a	prob.solv.	symbolic	16a	principle	symbolic
12b	principle	iconic-symbolic	16b	principle	symbolic
			16c	principle	symbolic
			16d	principle	symbolic
Part 2			16e	principle	symbolic
12c	principle	symbolic	16f	principle	symbolic
12d	prob.solv.	symbolic	16g	principle	symbolic
12e	prob.solv.	symbolic	16h	prob.solv.	symbolic
12h	prob.solv.	symbolic	17a	prob.solv.	iconic
9h	principle	symbolic	17b	principle	iconic
9i	prob.solv.	symbolic	17c	principle	symbolic
10d	principle	iconic	17d	prob.solv.	iconic
10e	principle	iconic	*Part 4*		
10f	principle	symbolic			
10g	principle	symbolic	17e	prob.solv.	iconic
13a	principle	iconic	17f	prob.solv.	iconic
13b	principle	iconic	17g	prob.solv.	symbolic
13c	principle	symbolic	17h	prob.solv.	iconic
13d	principle	iconic	17i	concept	iconic
13e	principle	symbolic	17j	principle	iconic
14a	concept	symbolic	17k	concept	iconic
14b	concept	symbolic	18a	prob.solv.	symbolic
14c	principle	symbolic	18b	principle	iconic
10h	principle	symbolic	18c	prob.solv.	symbolic

Individual SAMI Profile

The following is a suggested format for obtaining a diagnostic profile of an individual student's performance on the SAMI. The profile gives the teacher an "at-a-glance" picture of the student's strengths and weaknesses in areas tapped by SAMI.

Individual SAMI Profile

Name _____ Grade in School _____

Part 1: Grades K–2

CA _____ MA _____ Date _____

Step 1: Circle incorrect items.

A. Proximity, Spatial Relations, Size

1a,1b,2a,2b,2c,2d,2e,2f,3a,3b,

B. Numeration

4a,4b,4c,7a,7c

C. Cardinality, Classification, Equivalence, Nonequivalence

5a,5b,6a,6b,7b,8a,8b,8c

D. Operations on Whole Numbers

9a,9b,9c,9d,9e,9f,9g,10a,10b,10c, 11a,11b,11c,11d,11e,11f,11g,12a, 12b

Step 2: Count the number of correct items (not circled) for each group.

Step 3: To find percent of items correct within each group, first circle number of items correct in each box below, and then circle equivalent percent correct.

A.

No. of Items Correct	Equi. % Correct
10	100
9	90
8	80
7	70
6	60
5	50
4	40
3	30
2	20
1	10

B.

# Correct	% Correct
5	100
4	80
3	60
2	40
1	20

C.

# Correct	% Correct
8	100
7	88
6	75
5	63
4	50
3	38
2	25
1	13

D.

No. of Items Correct	Approx. % Correct	# Correct	Approx. % Correct
19	100	9	48
18	95	8	42
17	90	7	37
16	85	6	32
15	80	5	27
14	75	4	21
13	69	3	16
12	64	2	11
11	58	1	5
10	53		

Step 4: On Chart below, graph percentage correct in each group to show the child's strengths and weaknesses.

Percent of Items Correct

100
80
60
40
20
0

A. Proximity, Spatial Relations, Size

B. Numeration

C. Cardinality, Classification, Equivalence, Nonequivalence

D. Operations on Whole Numbers

135

Individual SAMI Profile

Part 2: Grades 3–4

Step 1: Circle incorrect items.

Name _____

CA _____ MA _____

Grade in School _____

Date _____

A. Cardinality, Classification, Equivalence, Nonequivalence

6a, 6b, 7b, 8a, 8b, 8c

B. Operations on Whole Numbers

9a, 9b, 9c, 9d, 9e, 9f, 9g, 9h, 9i,10a,10b,10c,10d,10e,10f,10g, 10h,10i,11a,11b,11c,11d,11e,11f, 11g,12a,12b,12c,12d,12e,12f,12g, 12h,13a,13b,13c,13d,13e

C. Prime Numbers

14a, 14b, 14c

D. Fractions

15a,15b,15c,15d,15e, 15f,15g,15h,15i

Step 2: Count the number of correct items (not circled) for each group.

Step 3: To find percent of items correct within each group, first circle number of items correct in each box below, and then circle equivalent percent correct.

A.

# Corr.	% Corr.
6	100
5	85
4	68
3	51
2	34
1	17

B.

# Corr.	% Corr.	# Corr.	% Corr.	# Corr.	% Corr.	# Corr.	% Corr.
38	100	30	79	20	52	10	26
37	97	29	75	19	49	9	23
36	95	28	73	18	47	8	21
35	91	27	70	17	44	7	18
34	89	26	68	16	42	6	16
33	87	25	65	15	39	5	13
32	84	24	62	14	36	4	10
31	81	23	60	13	34	3	8
		22	57	12	31	2	5
		21	55	11	29	1	3

C.

# Corr.	% Corr.
3	100
2	66
1	33

D.

# Corr.	% Corr.
9	100
8	88
7	77
6	66
5	55
4	44
3	33
2	22
1	11

Step 4: On Chart below, graph percentage correct in each group to show the child's strengths and weaknesses.

Percent of Items Correct

100
80
60
40
20
0

A. Cardinality, Classification, Equivalence, Nonequivalence   B. Operations on Whole Numbers   C. Prime Numbers   D. Fractions

136

Name _____ Grade in School _____

CA _____ MA _____ Date _____

Individual SAMI Profile

Part 3: Grades 5–6

Step 1: Circle incorrect items.

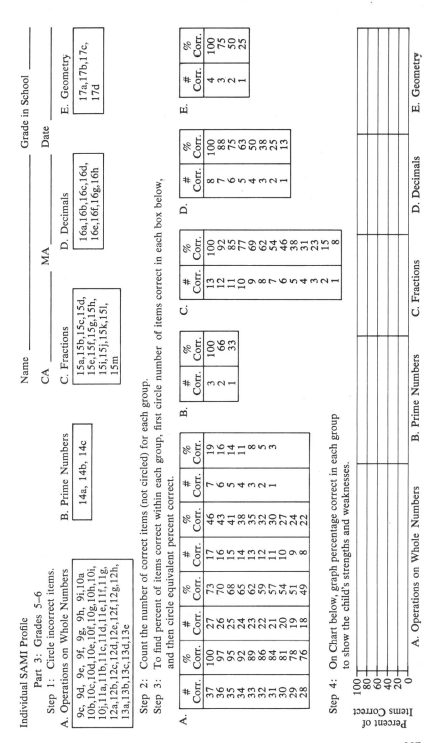

A. Operations on Whole Numbers	B. Prime Numbers	C. Fractions	D. Decimals	E. Geometry
9c, 9d, 9e, 9f, 9g, 9h, 9i,10a 10b,10c,10d,10e,10f,10g,10h,10i, 10j,11a,11b,11c,11d,11e,11f,11g, 12a,12b,12c,12d,12e,12f,12g,12h, 13a,13b,13c,13d,13e	14a, 14b, 14c	15a,15b,15c,15d, 15e,15f,15g,15h, 15i,15j,15k,15l, 15m	16a,16b,16c,16d, 16e,16f,16g,16h	17a,17b,17c, 17d

Step 2: Count the number of correct items (not circled) for each group.

Step 3: To find percent of items correct within each group, first circle number of items correct in each box below, and then circle equivalent percent correct.

A.

# Corr.	% Corr.	# Corr.	% Corr.	# Corr.	% Corr.
37	100	17	46	7	19
36	97	16	43	6	16
35	95	15	41	5	14
34	92	14	38	4	11
33	89	13	35	3	8
32	86	12	32	2	5
31	84	11	30	1	3
30	81	10	27		
29	78	9	24		
28	76	8	22		

B.

# Corr.	% Corr.
3	100
2	66
1	33

C.

# Corr.	% Corr.
13	100
12	92
11	85
10	77
9	69
8	62
7	54
6	46
5	38
4	31
3	23
2	15
1	8

D.

# Corr.	% Corr.
8	100
7	88
6	75
5	63
4	50
3	38
2	25
1	13

E.

# Corr.	% Corr.
4	100
3	75
2	50
1	25

Step 4: On Chart below, graph percentage correct in each group to show the child's strengths and weaknesses.

Percent of Items Correct: 100 80 60 40 20 0

A. Operations on Whole Numbers B. Prime Numbers C. Fractions D. Decimals E. Geometry

137

Individual SAMI Profile

Part 4: Grades 7–8

Name _____

Grade in School _____

CA _____ MA _____ Date _____

Step 1: Circle incorrect items.

A. Operations on Whole Number	B. Prime Numbers	C. Fractions	D. Decimals	E. Geometry	F. Probability and Statistics
13a,13b,13c,13d,13e	14a,14b,14c	15a,15b,15c,15d,15e, 15f,15g,15h,15i,15j, 15k,15l,15m	16a,16b,16c,16d, 16e,16f,16g,16h	17a,17b,17c,17d, 17e,17f,17g,17h, 17i,17j,17k	18a, 18b, 18c

Step 2: Count the number of correct items (not circled) for each group.

Step 3: To find percent of items correct within each group, first circle number of items correct in each box below, and then circle equivalent percent correct.

A.
No. of Items Correct	Equi. % Correct
5	100
4	80
3	60
2	40
1	20

B.
# Correct	% Correct
3	100
2	66
1	33

C.
# Correct	% Correct
13	100
12	92
11	85
10	77
9	69
8	62
7	54
6	46
5	38
4	31
3	23
2	15
1	8

D.
# Correct	% Correct
8	100
7	88
6	75
5	63
4	50
3	38
2	25
1	13

E.
# Correct	% Correct
11	100
10	91
9	82
8	73
7	64
6	55
5	46
4	36
3	27
2	18
1	9

F.
# Correct	% Correct
3	100
2	66
1	33

Step 4: On Chart below, graph percentage correct in each group to show the child's strengths and weaknesses.

Percent of Correct Items

100
80
60
40
20
0

A. Operations on Whole Numbers	B. Prime Numbers	C. Fractions	D. Decimals	E. Geometry	F. Probability and Statistics

138

Class SAMI Profile

The teacher may wish to know how the class as a whole achieved on each of the performance objectives that underlie the SAMI items. Following is a suggested summary sheet for showing the number of students who missed specific items.

Class SAMI Profile

Part 1: Grades K–2

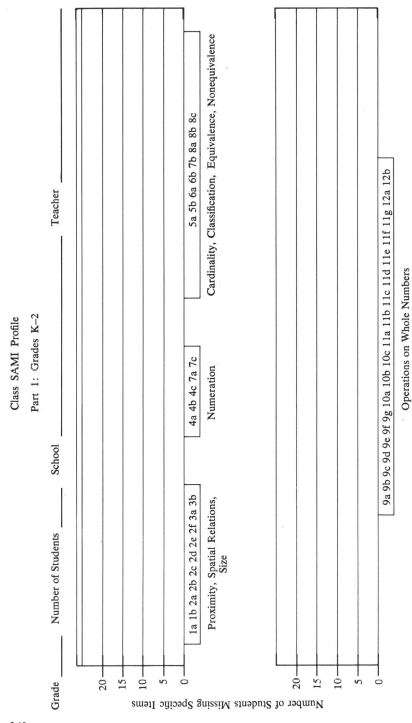

Grade _____ Number of Students _____ School _____ Teacher _____

1a 1b 2a 2b 2c 2d 2e 2f 3a 3b
Proximity, Spatial Relations, Size

4a 4b 4c 7a 7c
Numeration

5a 5b 6a 6b 7b 8a 8b 8c
Cardinality, Classification, Equivalence, Nonequivalence

9a 9b 9c 9d 9e 9f 9g 10a 10b 10c 11a 11b 11c 11d 11e 11f 11g 12a 12b
Operations on Whole Numbers

Number of Students Missing Specific Items

140

Class SAMI Profile

Part 2: Grades 3–4

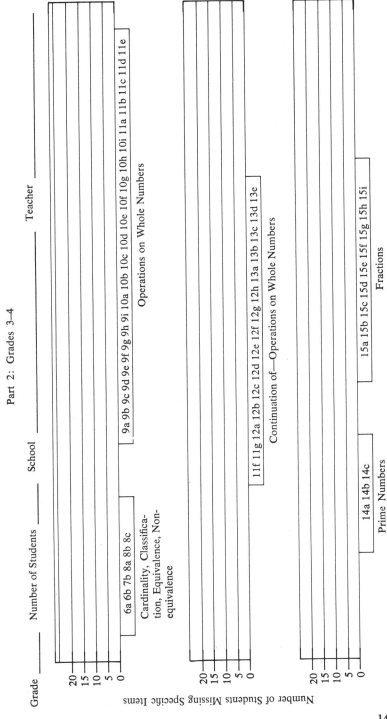

Grade _____ Number of Students _____ School _____ Teacher

6a 6b 7b 8a 8b 8c — Cardinality, Classification, Equivalence, Non-equivalence

9a 9b 9c 9d 9e 9f 9g 9h 9i 10a 10b 10c 10d 10e 10f 10g 10h 10i 11a 11b 11c 11d 11e — Operations on Whole Numbers

11f 11g 12a 12b 12c 12d 12e 12f 12g 12h 13a 13b 13c 13d 13e — Continuation of—Operations on Whole Numbers

14a 14b 14c — Prime Numbers

15a 15b 15c 15d 15e 15f 15g 15h 15i — Fractions

Number of Students Missing Specific Items

Class SAMI Profile

Part 3: Grades 5–6

Grade _____ Number of Students _____ School _____ Teacher

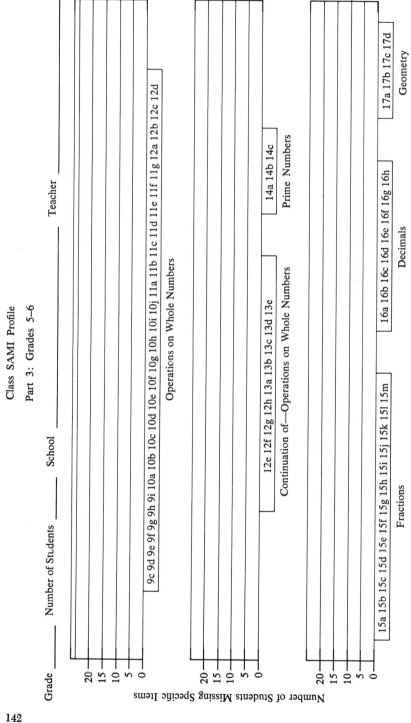

9c 9d 9e 9f 9g 9h 9i 10a 10b 10c 10d 10e 10f 10g 10h 10i 10j 11a 11b 11c 11d 11e 11f 11g 12a 12b 12c 12d

Operations on Whole Numbers

12e 12f 12g 12h 13a 13b 13c 13d 13e

Continuation of—Operations on Whole Numbers

14a 14b 14c

Prime Numbers

15a 15b 15c 15d 15e 15f 15g 15h 15i 15j 15k 15l 15m

Fractions

16a 16b 16c 16d 16e 16f 16g 16h

Decimals

17a 17b 17c 17d

Geometry

Number of Students Missing Specific Items

Class SAMI Profile

Part 4: Grades 7–8

Grade _____ Number of Students _____ School _____ Teacher _____

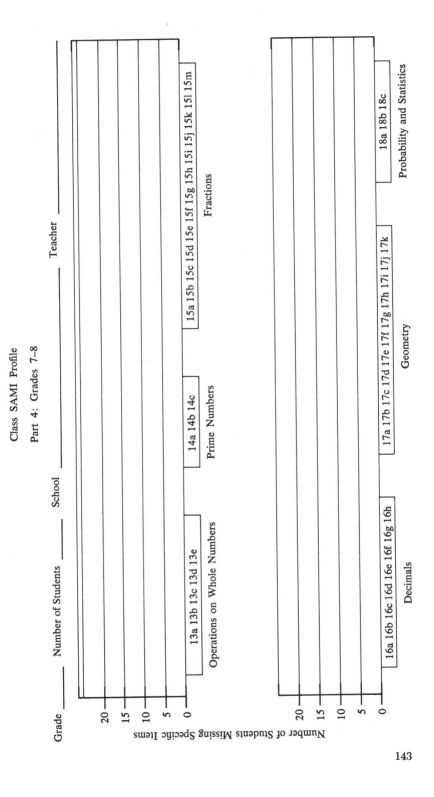

13a 13b 13c 13d 13e
Operations on Whole Numbers

14a 14b 14c
Prime Numbers

15a 15b 15c 15d 15e 15f 15g 15h 15i 15j 15k 15l 15m
Fractions

16a 16b 16c 16d 16e 16f 16g 16h
Decimals

17a 17b 17c 17d 17e 17f 17g 17h 17i 17j 17k
Geometry

18a 18b 18c
Probability and Statistics

Number of Students Missing Specific Items

20 15 10 5 0

20 15 10 5 0

143

Teacher-made tests are effective diagnostic tools.

Analysis of basic arithmetic errors serve as an aid in diagnosing where a child is in need of reteaching.

Indepth case studies of children in particular provide insights into children in general.

Form instructional groups by clustering children according to their rates of development as assessed by Piagetian tasks and by other appropriate tools.

144

Part 3

Synthesis of Diagnostic Teaching Cycle

12

An Analysis of Some Common Errors Children Make in Elementary School Mathmetics (15)

The following chart includes examples of common errors in elementary school mathematics and analyses of the reasoning for them. This chart will serve as an aid in diagnosing where the child is in need of reteaching.

	Analysis	*Example*
1.	Lacks mastery of basic addition facts.	$\begin{array}{r} 3\ 2 \\ +4\ 3 \\ \hline 7\ 4 \end{array}$
2.	Lacks mastery of basic subtraction facts.	$\begin{array}{r} 3\ 8 \\ -2\ 5 \\ \hline 1\ 2 \end{array}$
3.	Lacks mastery of basic multiplication facts.	$\begin{array}{r} 3\ 2 \\ \times\ \ \ 3 \\ \hline 86 \end{array}$
4.	Lacks mastery of basic division facts.	$35 \div 5 = 6$ $\begin{array}{r} 6 \\ 9\overline{)\ 56} \\ -56 \\ \hline 0 \end{array}$

147

| *Analysis* | *Example* |

5. Subtracts incorrectly within the division algorithm.

$$
\begin{array}{r}
3)\ \ 73\ \text{rem}\ 1 \\
70) \\
3\overline{/230} \\
-21 \\
\hline
10 \longleftarrow \\
-9 \\
\hline
1
\end{array}
$$

6. Error in addition of partial product.

$$
\begin{array}{r}
432 \\
\times 57 \\
\hline
3\ 0\ 24 \\
21\ 6\ 0 \\
24\ 0\ 24
\end{array}
$$

7. Does not complete addition:
   a. Does not write renamed number.

$$
\begin{array}{r}
85 \\
+43 \\
\hline
28
\end{array}
$$

   b. Leaves out numbers in column addition.

$$
\begin{array}{r}
4 \\
8 \\
2 \longleftarrow \\
+3 \\
\hline
15
\end{array}
$$

8. Rewrites a numeral without computing.

$$
\begin{array}{r}
72 \\
+15 \\
\hline
77 \\
32 \\
\times\ \ 3 \\
\hline
36
\end{array}
$$

9. Does not complete subtraction.

$$
\begin{array}{r}
582 \\
-\ 35 \\
\hline
47
\end{array}
$$

Analysis	*Example*

10. Does not complete division because of incomplete subtraction.

$$\begin{array}{r} 1)\ 41 \\ 40) \\ 7\overline{)3\ 9\ 7} \\ -2\ 8\ 0 \\ \hline 7 \\ 7 \\ \hline \end{array}$$

11. Fails to complete division; stops at first partial quotient.

$$\begin{array}{r} 50 \\ 7\overline{)370} \\ 350 \\ \end{array}$$

12. Fails to complete division; leaves remainder equal to or greater than divisor.

$$\begin{array}{r} 80\ \text{rem}\ 9 \\ 9\overline{)729} \\ 720 \\ \hline 9 \\ \end{array}$$

13. Does not complete multiplication within division algorithm.

$$\begin{array}{r} 1)\ 201\ \text{rem}\ 3 \\ 200) \\ 3\overline{)603} \\ 600 \\ \hline 3 \\ \end{array}$$

14. Does not add by bridging endings—should think $5 + 9 = 14$, so $35 + 9 = 44$.

$$\begin{array}{r} 35 \\ +9 \\ \hline 33 \\ \end{array}$$

15. Lacks additive identity concept in addition.

$$\begin{array}{r} 35 \\ +20 \\ \hline 50 \\ \end{array}$$

16. Confuses multiplicative identity within addition operation.

$$\begin{array}{r} 71 \\ +13 \\ \hline 73 \\ \end{array}$$

Analysis	*Example*

17. Lacks additive identity concept in subtraction.

$$\begin{array}{r} 43 \\ -20 \\ \hline 20 \end{array}$$

18. Confuses role of zero in subtraction with role of zero in multiplication.

$$\begin{array}{r} 37 \\ -20 \\ \hline 10 \end{array}$$

19. Subtracts top digit from bottom digit whenever regrouping is involved with zero in minuend.

$$\begin{array}{r} 30 \\ -18 \\ \hline 28 \end{array}$$

20. Confuses role of zero in multiplication with multiplicative identity.

$$7 \times 0 = 7$$

21. Confuses place value of quotient by adding extra zero.

$$\begin{array}{r} 20 \\ 30\overline{)\ 60} \end{array}$$

22. Omits zero in quotient.

$$\begin{array}{r} 30 \text{ rem } 3 \\ 4\overline{)\ 1203} \\ 1200 \\ \hline 3 \end{array}$$

23. Lacks facility with addition algorithm:
    a. Adds units to units *and* tens;

$$\begin{array}{r} 37 \\ +\ \ 2 \\ \hline 59 \end{array}$$

   b. Adds tens to tens *and* hundreds;

$$\begin{array}{r} 342 \\ +\ 36 \\ \hline 678 \end{array}$$

| *Analysis* | *Example* |

c. Adds units to tens *and* hundreds;

$$
\begin{array}{r}
132 \\
+6 \\
\hline
798
\end{array}
$$

d. Is unable to add horizontally:

$$345 + 7 + 13 = 185$$

Thinks: $3 + 7 + 1 = 11$; writes 1

$$
\begin{array}{rll}
4 + 3 & = 7 \ (+\ 1\ \text{carried}) & 8 \\
5 & = 5 & 5 \\
\hline
& & 185
\end{array}
$$

May add zero to make sum
greater than largest addend: 1850.

24. Does not regroup units to tens.

$$
\begin{array}{r}
37 \\
+\ 25 \\
\hline
52
\end{array}
$$

25. Does not regroup tens to hundreds
(or hundreds to thousands).

$$
\begin{array}{r}
973 \\
+862 \\
\hline
735
\end{array}
$$

26. Regroups when unnecessary.

$$
\begin{array}{r}
43 \\
+\ 24 \\
\hline
77
\end{array}
$$

27. Writes regrouped tens digit in
units place, carries units digit
(writes the 1 and carries the 2
from "12").

$$
\begin{array}{r}
② \\
35 \\
+7 \\
\hline
51
\end{array}
$$

28. When there are fewer digits in
subtrahend:
a. subtracts units from units *and*
from tens (*and* hundreds);

$$
\begin{array}{r}
783 \\
-2 \\
\hline
561
\end{array}
$$

b. subtracts tens from tens *and*
hundreds.

$$
\begin{array}{r}
783 \\
-\ 23 \\
\hline
560
\end{array}
$$

Analysis	*Example*
29. Does not rename tens digit after regrouping.	$\begin{array}{r} 54 \\ -9 \\ \hline 55 \end{array}$
30. Does not rename hundreds digit after regrouping.	$\begin{array}{r} 532 \\ -181 \\ \hline 451 \end{array}$
31. Does not rename hundreds or tens when renaming units.	$\begin{array}{r} 906 \\ -238 \\ \hline 778 \end{array}$
32. Does not rename tens when zero is in tens place, although hundreds are renamed.	$\begin{array}{r} 803 \\ -478 \\ \hline 335 \end{array}$
33. When there are two zeroes in minuend, renames hundreds twice but does not rename tens.	$\begin{array}{r} 5 \\ \cancel{6}_{\,1\,1} \\ \cancel{7}00 \\ -326 \\ \hline 284 \end{array}$
34. Decreases hundreds digit by one when unnecessary.	$\begin{array}{r} 3\;7\;1 \\ -1\;3\;4 \\ \hline 1\;3\;7 \end{array}$
35. Uses units place factor as addend.	$\begin{array}{r} 32 \\ \times4 \\ \hline 126 \end{array}$
36. Adds regrouped number to tens but does not multiply.	$\begin{array}{r} 35 \\ \times7 \\ \hline 65* \end{array}$

$$* \; 7 \times \; 5 = 35;$$
$$30 + 30 = 60$$

Analysis	*Example*

37. Multiplies digits within one factor.

$$\begin{array}{r} 31 \\ \times \quad 4 \\ \hline 34* \end{array}$$

$$* \ 4 \times \ 1 = \ 4;$$
$$1 \times 30 = 30$$

38. Multiplies by only one number.

$$\begin{array}{r} 457 \\ \times \ 12 \\ \hline 914 \end{array}$$

39. "Carries" wrong number.

$$\begin{array}{r} 8 \\ 67 \\ \times \ 40 \\ \hline 3220 \end{array}$$

40. Does not multiply units times tens.

$$\begin{array}{r} 32 \\ \times \ 24 \\ \hline 648 \end{array}$$

41. Reverses divisor with dividend.

$$6\overline{)\ 30}\ \ \ ^{2\ *}$$

* Thinks $6 \div 3$ instead of $30 \div 6$

42. Does not regroup; treats each
    column as separate addition example.

$$\begin{array}{r} 23 \\ + \quad 8 \\ \hline 211 \end{array}$$

43. Subtracts smaller digit from
    larger at all times to avoid
    renaming.

$$\begin{array}{r} 273 \\ -639 \\ \hline 446 \end{array}$$

44. Does not add regrouped number.

$$\begin{array}{r} 37 \\ \times \quad 7 \\ \hline 219 \end{array}$$

Analysis	*Example*

45. Confuses place value in division:

$$\begin{array}{r} 1) \\ 200) \quad 201 \\ 3\overline{)6003} \end{array}$$

    a. Considers thousands divided by units as hundreds divided by units;

$$\begin{array}{r} 6000 \\ \hline 3 \\ 3 \\ \hline \end{array}$$

    b. records partial quotient as tens instead of units;

$$\begin{array}{r} 50) \\ 100) \quad 150 \\ 7\overline{)735} \\ -700 \\ \hline 35 \\ 35 \\ \hline \end{array}$$

    c. omits zero needed to show no units in quotient.

$$\begin{array}{r} 2 \text{ rem } 1 \\ 3\overline{)61} \\ 6 \\ \hline 1 \end{array}$$

46. Ignores remainder because:
    a. does not complete subtraction;
    b. does not *see* need for further computation;
    c. does not know what to do with "2" if subtraction occurs, so does not compute further.

$$\begin{array}{r} 80 \\ 7\overline{)562} \\ 560 \\ \hline \end{array}$$

13

Sample Lesson Plans and Some Suggestions for Remediation of Common Difficulties in Mathematics

Diagnosed Difficulties	Procedure	Evaluation
1. Writing digits—0 to 9.	Use all of the child's senses in teaching her. Use cut-out digits for the student to trace with her fingers. Use felt, sandpaper, clay for digits. Have her draw digits in sand.	Teacher says digit for child to write.
2. Writing numerals without reversing place value.	Practice left-right sequence. Review names of place value positions.	Teacher says numeral and has child record.
3. Adding with renaming.	a. Review place-value concept. Start at the concrete (enactive) level by having child combine five tongue depressors with nine. Bundle ten of the fourteen as one ten and there will be four ones left over.	Child will bundle ones as tens and ones.

155

Diagnosed Difficulty	*Procedure*	*Evaluation*

b. Have child record as follows:

tens	ones
	9
+	5
1	4

Child will compute using place value chart as aid.

c. Then move to the symbolic level using numerals:

$$\begin{array}{r} 25 \\ +9 \\ \hline 14 \\ 20 \\ \hline 34 \end{array}$$

Then introduce the standard algorithm:

$$\begin{array}{r} 25 \\ +9 \\ \hline 34 \end{array}$$

Child will add with renaming units as one ten and so many units.

4. Subtracting with renaming

a. Review addition with renaming at the enactive level as in Procedure 3a. Use the same example but now subtract (25−9). Guide child to see that she has two bundles of ten and five ones:

Child will regroup two tens and five units as one ten and fifteen units.

TENS   UNITS

///////// //////

/////////

Diagnosed Difficulty	*Procedure*	*Evaluation*

	b. Have child record this in place value chart:
	
	   Tens *Ones*
	
	    2 5
		Child will record concrete situations correctly

	c. Next have child take nine tongue depressors away. She sees she does not have enough to do this. She is now in a problem-solving situation. Guide her to take rubber band off one bundle of ten and count them all out as fifteen units. Let her place these in the units position and remove nine tongue depressors.	Child will subtract by using concrete objects
	d. Have child record problem in place value chart and compute.	Child will subtract with renaming.

tens	units
2	5
–	9
1	15
–	9
1	6

5. Concept of Additive Identity: $n + o = n$	a. Combine a set (A) with the null (empty) set to show that the number property of these two sets is the same as for the first set (A).	Child combines sets with null set to get cardinal number property of first set.

Diagnosed Difficulty	*Procedure*	*Evaluation*
	b. Child needs practice in computing this: $4 + 0 = 4$, $9 + 0 = 9$, $73 + 0 = 73$, etc.	
6. Concept of Multiplicative Identity: $n \times 1 = n$	a. Use iconic level: 1×5	Child can describe multiplication from diagram.
	b. Use symbolic level: $3 \times \Box = 3$ $3 \times 1 = \Box$ $3 \times 1 =$ $\Box \times 1 = 3$	Child fills in blanks
7. Multiplying with renaming: 2×36	a. Use distributive property: $2 \times 36 = 2 \times (30 + 6)$ $= (2 \times 30) + (2 \times 6)$ $= 60 + 12$ $= 72$ Then compare this algorithm with vertical algorithm: $\begin{array}{ccc} 36 = & 30 & 6 \\ \times 2 & \times 2 & \times 2 \\ \hline 12 & 60 & + 12 \\ 60 & & \\ \hline 72 = & & 72 \end{array}$	Child will multiply with renaming.

Diagnosed Difficulty	*Procedure*	*Evaluation*

b. Use picture mode:
$$6 \times 12$$

6×12

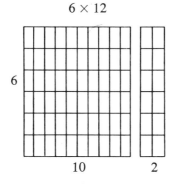

$$6 \times 12 = 6 \times (10 + 2)$$
$$= (6 \times 10) +$$
$$(6 \times 2)$$
$$= 60 + 12$$
$$= 72$$

8. Renaming equivalent fractions.

a. Enactive level. Compare equivalent regions using cutouts.

Child can manipulate factional pieces.

Model Whole

$\frac{1}{2}$	

Cut second whole into halves

$\frac{1}{4}$			

Cut third whole into fourths

$\frac{1}{8}$							

Cut fourth whole into eighths

Diagnosed Difficulty	*Procedure*	*Evaluation*

Guide child to place four eighths over $1/2$ and two fourths over $1/2$. This helps her to attain the concept of equivalent fractions.

b. Iconic level.
   Compare equivalent regions:
   $$1/2 = 2/4 = 4/8$$

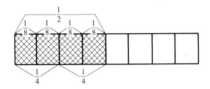

Child can compare equivalent fractions from diagrams.

c. Symbolic level: Use concept of multiplicative identity.
   $$1/2 \times 1 = \square\, /4$$
   $$1/2 \times 2/2 = 2/4$$
   Think $2 \times \square = 4$. This gives you cue for special name for 1. In this case $2/2$.

Child can rename equivalent fractions

9. Adding fractions with same denominators: $1/3 + 1/3 =$

a. Use enactive level (see 8a). Have child combine $1/4$ and $1/4$ pieces of whole and count to obtain two fourths $(2/4)$.

Child combines fractional pieces

b. Use this algorithm:
   $$1/4 + 1/4 = \frac{1 + 1}{4} = 2/4$$

Child computes using this algorithm

10. Adding fractions with different denominators: $1/4 + 1/2 =$

Prerequisite is multiplying fraction by fraction:
   $$1/2 \times 2/2 = 2/4$$

Diagnosed Difficulty	*Procedure*	*Evaluation*
	a. Enactive level: Use fractional pieces (see 8a) $$1/4 = 1/4$$	Child combines fractional parts to obtain $\frac{3}{4}$.

$$1/2 = 2/4$$

b. Symbolic level:
$$1/4 = 1/4$$
$$*+1/2 = 2/4$$
$$\overline{3/4}$$

Child adds fractions with different denominators.

* Renaming 1/2 as 2/4

$$\frac{1}{2} \times \frac{2}{\boxed{2}} = \frac{2}{4}$$

Child must think 2 times what number yields 4? This gives her a special name for 1 in the form $\frac{2}{2}$. She then finds the equivalent of $\frac{1}{2}$ in fourths by multiplying the fractions $\frac{1}{2}$ by $\frac{2}{2}$.

| 11. Adding decimal fractions. | Concentrate on writing numerals in vertical position: $$\begin{array}{r} 5.06 \\ .789 \\ +19.1 \\ \hline \end{array}$$ Guide children to place decimal dots under each other and to either fill in empty spaces with zeros or round to the least precise addend. Then, they add as with whole numbers. Use of graph paper helps align digits. | Child adds decimal fractions. |

Diagnosed Difficulty	*Procedure*	*Evaluation*
12. Multiplying decimal fractions: $.5 \times .03 =$	a. Rename $.5 \times .03$ to $(5 \times 3) \times (.1 \times .01)$. Use associative properties: $5 \times .1 \times 3 \times .01$. Multiply whole numbers: $5 \times 3 = 15$. Multiply place values: tenth $\times$ hundredths $=$ thousandths. Decide on number of decimal places thousandths take up: *tenths hundredths thousandths* Show number of places needed in this way: . ____ ____ ____ Then write in face value (15) so that the last place is filled: . _1_ _5_ . Fill in empty places with zeros: . _0_ _1_ _5_ . b. Guide child to notice that number of decimal places in product is the sum of number of decimal places in factors: (places: $1 + 2 = 3$) $.5 \times .03 = .0\ \underline{1}\ \underline{5}$	Child uses this form: $.5 \times .03 =$ $5 \times .1 \times 3 \times .01 =$ $(5 \times 3) \times (.1 \times .01) =$ $15 \times .001 =$ $.0\ \underline{1}\ \underline{5}$
13. Dividing decimal fraction by decimal fraction: $.25 \div .5 =$ ☐	a. Write the division as a fraction. $.25/.5$ b. Multiply the denominator by the multiple of ten that will yield a whole number: $\dfrac{.25}{.5} \times \dfrac{10}{10} = \dfrac{2.50}{5.0} = \dfrac{2.5}{5}$ c. Divide the face values: $25 \div 5 = 5$	Divide decimals

Diagnosed Difficulty   *Procedure*   *Evaluation*

d. Insert the same number of decimal places in the quotient as are now in the dividend.

$$.25 \div .5 = \square$$

(multiply by 10)

$$2.5 \div 5 = .5$$

14

Synthesis of
Diagnostic Teaching Cycle—
Or Pulling It All Together

The synthesis model presented in Figure 14 has evolved from expressed needs of students in Diagnostic Teaching of Elementary School Mathematics courses as well as from instructors using the first edition of this text. Listed are diagnostic hierarchies for considering a child's needs and developmental levels (Maslow and Piaget); for evaluating item complexity and the nature of the curriculum (Bloom's Cognitive Domain Taxonomy and Reisman's modification of Brownell/Gagne's types of learning); and for selecting modes of representing content to be learned (Bruner).

Thus far, these hierarchies have been considered vertically. In order to synthesize the Diagnostic Teaching Cycle model, we must now look horizontally across the individual theories and taxonomies. The slopes between and among hierarchies yield insights that explain difficulties in mathematics learning.

One such insight involves learning to *recall and reproduce the digits representing numbers zero through nine.* This task is graphed across the three hierarchies representing mode of representation, type of learning, and item complexity in Figure 15.

Notice that this task is an arbitary association and involves recall, both of which are minimum in meaningfulness; it is at the same time symbolic in nature. Symbols such as numerals and written words yield the least sensory information to the learner. These observations are clues to the teacher for instruction and for placement of curriculum. The inappropriateness of this task for most kindergarten and for many first-grade children is further highlighted when we consider where most of these children are located in terms of Piaget's developmental theory.

165

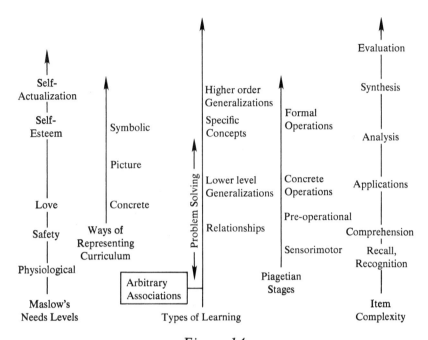

Figure 14

Model for Synthesizing Diagnostic Tools

Most children at these grade levels are pre-operational in their thinking. They are not yet ready to handle logical or abstract symbol systems. Although they can learn symbols rotely if given enough drill, is such time on task economical when these symbols will be lacking in meaningful referents? The slopes among hierarchies in Figure 15 point out that this task is simultaneously at the highest and lowest levels of abstracting. Such observations help the teacher select curriculum and instructional techniques that mesh with the learner's rate of development.

One type of strategy for synthesizing diagnostic tools presented in this book is to graph positions of objectives for selected SAMI items on the appropriate hierarchies in Figure 14 that the child (or children if group administered) missed. Then judge whether there is an incongruent relationship among the line slopes. You may also wish to do the same with objectives for selected items answered correctly. Once such strengths and incongruences are identified, you are able to develop objectives for an alternative instructional program.

Another strategy for viewing the hierarchies horizontally is to start with the child's needs level (Maslow) or cognitive development (Piaget). Then select tasks that are consistent with one or both of these.

In viewing Figure 14 be aware that the horizontal positioning of levels

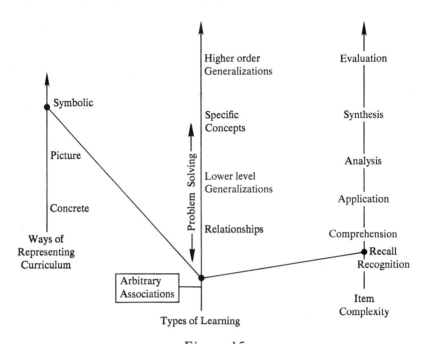

Figure 15

Analysis of Task Involving Writing Digits 0 to 9*

across hierarchies is not meant to represent fixed, compatible positions. For example, an *analysis* task may also involve *problem solving* and may at the same time be presented in a *concrete* way. For a child performing *formal operational* thinking who has at least satisfied personal *safety needs,* such a task is probably appropriate.

The diagnostic tools presented in this book may also be synthesized into a structure to organize your mathematics class for differential instruction. For example, you may administer an assessment such as the SAMI, your own teacher—made test, or a standardized mathematics test. If the SAMI is used, children may be grouped by analyzing the class profile (see pages 139–143) and individual profiles (see pages 134–138). Form instructional groups by clustering children according to their rates of development as assessed by the Piagetian tasks and then by the items missed on the SAMI. Evaluate these items across hierarchies as shown in Figures 14 and 15. Then develop differential programs of instruction for groups of four to eight children who have similar needs in view of their individual profiles. The instructional groups change as children demonstrate an understanding of relationships that underlie selected tasks.

---

* See SAMI item 4a, page 114.

15

Mini-Case Studies

The case studies presented serve to emphasize the complexities involved in diagnostic teaching of elementary school mathematics. They also provide the teacher with insights into the kinds of questions that need to be asked in order to assess a student's performance in mathematics. In many instances the regular classroom teacher will need to seek out the aid of a specialist in individual intelligence testing, one who understands the peculiarities in learning within children who have various learning discrepancies; one who can provide medical information about a child; one who can provide a total picture of the child in various academic, social, and familial settings; and one who can help the classroom teacher interpret and bridge the information that is provided by these "experts." How a child learns and what goes on during those learning processes is still very much a puzzle. However, children are in schools, they need to learn, and we as teachers must use the knowledge and educational technologies that we DO have to provide the optimal learning environments for the learner.

Mini-Case
Study 1

The first case discussed is a high school grade level youth who is operating at the middle school grade level in mathematics. The question of whether or not he is an underachiever is confounded by the fact that his subtest scores on the Wechsler Adult Intelligence Scale (WAIS) showed a wide scatter. In such a case total IQ score may not reflect his XGE and may be misleading. In cases where there are wide discrepancies among subtest scores they mask possible learning disabilities that may

169

prevent a child from performing at an expectancy level derived from the total score.

Fred, a friendly, cooperative student, seemed at ease in the testing situation except for heavy breathing as he worked items that he said were "hard." His performance on the SAMI, Part 4: Grades 7–8, showed a lack of readiness for high school mathematics.

Fred demonstrated some strengths in mathematics. He used the following mathematics relationships and ideas correctly during the diagnostic session: prime numbers; renaming a number as a product of its factors; fraction concepts; probability concepts at the most elementary level; descriptive statistics such as reading and interpreting graphs; multiplicative identity; and the multiplicative inverse idea.

Specific areas of weakness that were identified during the diagnostic session include the following: fraction operations ($\times$, $\div$, $+$, $-$); decimal concepts; decimal operations; metric system; measures of geometric figures; topological relations; transformations; transitive property as applied to identifying sets of equivalent fractions; distributive property of multiplication over addition applied to mixed numbers, and to algebraic expressions; operations with complex fractions; angle measures; role of multiplicative identity in dividing a number by itself (Fred computed $7 \div 7 = 0$ and did not recognize that division by zero is undefined in the problem $5/7 \div 1/7 = 5/0$); and graphing ordered pairs on an x/y axis. It was also noticed that use of a number line was an inappropriate instructional tool for Fred. The abstract representation of number relations seemed to cause him more confusion than help.

Mini-Case
Study 2

Martin is ten years old (10.0) and is in the fourth grade (4.2). The California Test of Mental Maturity (Short Form) was administered when he was nine years and three months old. This test yielded an IQ score of 95. The Stanford Diagnostic Arithmetic Test, Level 1, was administered in November. On Test 1 (Concepts), Martin's grade score was 3.5 his grade score for Test 2 (Computation) was 4.0.

Examples of Answers Martin Gave

1. In answering an item requiring that he give the numerals which come just before and just after 200, his responses were 119 and 211.

2. Martin correctly answered the questions involving counting forward by twos and fives but missed the ones in which he had to go backwards.
3. Martin's answers to naming points on a number line were consistently incorrect by one.
4. Martin was unable to name fractions shown on a number line.

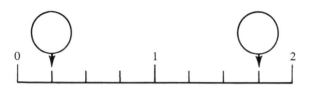

5. Martin gave the following answer in the Computation Part:
$$8 + 7 = 8 + \boxed{} + 5. \qquad \boxed{} = 75$$
6. Martin missed those questions dealing with interpreting and writing numerals. For example, one answer was 24 instead of 2040.
7. When asked to count by tens or twenties, Martin did not begin with the first number in the sequence. Instead, he went from 15 to 20 and then continued counting by tens. He did the same thing when asked to begin with 16 and count by twenties. He went first to 20 and then counted 40, 60, 80.
8. Martin subtracted 5 from 11 and got 4.
9. In multiplication involving renaming, he added in the renamed tens before multiplying.

Mini-Case
Study 3

Josephine is nine years and five months old (9.5) and is in the fourth grade (4.0). Her IQ is 119. Her Arithmetic Achievement scores were 4.2 for Concepts and 3.6 for Computation.

Examples of Answers Josephine Gave

1. In associating numbers with points on a number line, she missed three of the four examples because she could not discriminate between the points.
2. In multiplication and division, she missed problems involving the number 9.

3. She missed all division examples involving a two- or three-place number divided by a two- place number.
4. Josephine answered 20 for this problem:

She said, "I looked at the dots and saw there were 4 sets of 5 dots. Oh, I see—one set only has three in it."
5. Her answer to $8 + 7 = 8 + \boxed{} + 5$ was 23. She said, "I added $8 + 7 + 8$ and got 23."

Mini-Case
Study 4

Robert is in the second month of fourth grade and is nine years and four months old. His IQ was found to be 107.

His scores on the Stanford Diagnostic Arithmetic Test (SDAT) were 2.9 for Concepts and 3.4 for Computation. Following are some of the items he missed and Robert's responses:

1.

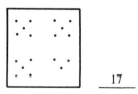

2. Which multiplications are shown by the arrangement of the dots?

```
. . . . .
. . . . .
. . . . .
. . . . .
```

1×20
20×1
4×5

$$\overset{\displaystyle 5 \times 4}{\underset{\displaystyle 10 \times 2}{\boxed{2 \times 10}}}$$

3. Which multiplication is shown on the line?

4.

5. Count by twenties. Start with 16.

    16, 18, 20, 22, 26

   Count by tens. Start with 15.

    15, 20, 25, 30, 35

6. Five ones, and six tens = 56

   Five ones, three hundreds, no tens = 530

   Six tens and twelve ones = 612

7.
```
  354      897      117      102      110      858      500       95
  +60     -417      -62      -81      -29     -139     -421       ×2
 ─────    ─────    ─────    ─────    ─────    ─────    ─────    ─────
  614       48      155      181       99      721      121      200

  204               31                12                         18
  × 3              ×23               ×40                      2/ 9
 ─────            ─────             ─────
  632               93                40
```

8. Robert answered these with much difficulty:

```
       2              8              31              21
    3/ 6           2/ 16          3/ 93          2/ 124
       6             16               9
      ──             ──              ──
                                      3
                                      3
```

Analysis of Mini-Case Studies

Analysis of Case Study 1

Fred would benefit from a basic elementary mathematics curriculum, presented concretely so that he can manipulate objects that serve as a physical model for mathematical relationships. Field axioms are a necessary prerequisite for his further work in mathematics. During the diagnostic session Fred showed he could learn such field axioms as the commutative and associative properties for addition and for multiplication, the distributive property of multiplication over addition, the additive identity and additive inverse relationships, the inverse element for multiplication, and the closure idea. However, he should have these ideas presented to him at the concrete level, rather than with pictures or equations only.

The use of a hand calculator might be useful for basic computations so that Fred can use his energy on the problem solving rather than on the mechanics of the computations. It was noted during the mathematics testing that his energy level dropped considerably. He appeared exhausted from his hard work. Fred seemed to enjoy some very basic probability tasks such as predicting results of coin tosses or predicting the color of a sock picked from a bag holding three white and one yellow sock.

Fred's mathematics might be related to budgeting, measuring surfaces, and reading scaled blueprints—these types of activities relate to real world situations.

Fred needs to engage in learning experiences related to his mathematics weaknesses. Even though he is of high school age, he still needs concrete activities from which he must be guided to abstract the underlying mathematical idea.

Analysis of Case Study 2

To find whether or not Martin may be considered an underachiever, first find his Expected Grade Equivalent Score (XGE). By performing the steps listed on page 50, we find the difference of XGE range is $4.7 - 3.7 = 1.0$ (see step a). This difference is multiplied by .7 which is the number of months beyond the lower age range of 9.0 years to 10.0 years since Martin is 9.7 years old (see step b). This product ($.7 \times 1.0 = .7$) is then added to the lower limit of Martin's XGE in the expectancy table, and we find his $XGE = 4.4$ ($3.7 + .7 = 4.4$, see step c).

Martin's arithmetic achievement score of 3.5 for concepts is almost at the ten month role of thumb difference for identifying underachievers. However, the 4.0 Computation score is only four months below his predicted grade placement.

Since Martin's score in concepts indicated that he is a borderline underachiever, he was given the Piaget tasks described on pages 56–58 of this handbook. He performed some of the tasks correctly without hesitation, while he completed others only after much trial and error. These results indicate that Martin needs instruction at the concrete and picture levels to enable him to abstract mathematical concepts at his own rate.

Martin's responses to questions on concepts reveal that he is able to count by ones only when dealing with one- or two-digit numerals. This fact is probably attributable to a lack of understanding of place value.

Martin correctly answered questions involving counting forward but missed those in which he was to count backwards. This implies that Martin is at Gagne's verbal association level (little or no meaning) rather than at the conceptual level. He seems to respond to the previous numeral without knowing why a certain numeral comes next.

It is possible that Martin's inability to name points on a number line is due to a simple misunderstanding of where he is to start counting. Further questioning showed that he started counting "one" at the zero point:

Martin was also unable to name fractions correctly on a number line. This operation involves applying his knowledge of fractions and of the number line to a new situation (transfer). It is categorized as 3.00, Application, on Bloom's Taxonomy.

Martin's performance on Test 1B (Concepts: operations) seems to reveal his lack of understanding of various mathematical principles. For example, in his answer to $8 + 5 = 8 + \boxed{75} + 5$, it seems that he was looking for "cues" to help in obtaining the right answer rather than engaging in problem solving. Martin was behaving at Bloom's 1.00 (Recall of Knowledge) level, trying to remember how to do this type of example, rather than trying to comprehend (2.20 Comprehension, Interpretation) what was being asked.

Martin depends mainly on recall of arbitrary associations rather than on conceptual meanings. This conclusion was illustrated further when he subtracted $-\dfrac{\begin{array}{r}11\\5\end{array}}{4}$. He evidently subtracted the one from five to get four and regrouped the one ten and one one as eleven ones. However, when he was asked, "What is eleven minus five," he responded, "Six."

It appears that Martin's lack of understanding of place value and his lack of knowledge of the basic mathematical principles—such as the Commutative, Associative, Distributive, and Identity laws—indicate a good place to start his remediation program.

Analysis of Case Study 3

Josephine's XGE was found to be 5.65. Her Concept score of 4.2 and her Computation score of 3.6 place her in the underachiever range.

Many of Josephine's errors were careless. It must be noted that she has a very short attention span and is a hyperactive child. Her responses to errors attest to this flighty behavior: "I just guessed;" "I don't know;" "I don't know which place is which;" "I see, I should have circled 109;" "It should be 305, I just wasn't thinking;" "I got confused, I should have circled 3200;" "Well, $4 + 3 = 7$; I multiplied there instead of adding;" "I added instead of subtracting, how dumb."

Josephine's weaknesses fall mainly in the Application (Bloom's 3.00) problems where she must use abstracting abilities. Work with Piaget's classifying activities at the enactive level should help her.

Since Josephine has a short attention span and is a poor listener, it is suggested that the guided discovery method of instruction at the enactive level would motivate her most to become involved in learning.

Analysis of Case Study 4

Robert's expected grade equivalent is 4.8 His arithmetic scores on the SDAT were: Concepts, 2.9 and Computation, 3.4. Thus, Robert would be considered an underachiever, and he has definite weaknesses in mathematics that may lead to severe difficulty later on.

A suggested remedial program for Robert should enable him to grasp the meaning of a number through emphasis on sets, subsets, equivalence relations ($>$, $=$, $<$), and the meaning of the properties (Commutative, Associative, Distributive, Identities, Inverses, and Multiplying by Zero). He should work mainly at the enactive and iconic levels to give him a foundation for computation.

Robert's abundance of errors with addition, subtraction, multiplication, and division algorithms shows that he is not successful at Bloom's

Application level. Usually, work with the properties underlying the algorithms helps the student with weaknesses in computation skills.

The above mini-case studies comprise a brief model for analyzing a student's response in mathematics. An inspection of the mathematics content in terms of what types of learning are involved provides you with a profile of your student's weak areas. By using the various hierarchies, you analyze the mathematics in terms of its appropriateness to the student's cognitive structure. You then can determine if the student has the necessary prerequisites for the particular mathematics content to be learned. You are in a position to determine the best method of teaching a particular mathematics content. You can decide upon a didactic technique or a guided discovery approach. You may use concrete materials, pictures, or words and numerals. You may ask the student to recall a fact, to analyze a word problem, or to apply the Commutative Property for Addition. You now can diagnose whether a child is an underachiever or whether he is working at his predicted level of achievement.

The tools for employing a diagnostic strategy of teaching present techniques for detecting your student's weak areas in mathematics and provide structure for building Individual Educational Plans (IEP). The IEP developed for a particular child may be appropriate for several children in a classroom in terms of mathematical content.

References

1. Bloom, Benjamin S.; Engelhart, Max D.; Furst, Edward J.; Hill, Walker H.; and Krathwohl, David R. *Taxonomy of Educational Objectives Handbook I: Cognitive Domain.* New York: David McKay Co., 1956.

2. Brownell, William H., and Hendrickson, Gordon. "How Children Learn Information, Concepts, and Generalizations." *The Forty-ninth Yearbook of the National Society for the Study of Education, Part I.* Chicago: University of Chicago Press, 1950.

3. Bruner, J. S. *Toward a Theory of Instruction.* Cambridge: Harvard University Press, Belknap Press, 1963. Bruner has labeled three levels of representing information about the real world as "enactive," "iconic," and "symbolic." The enactive level is the first representation a child uses. It involves active involvement of the child and may be translated into an educational meaning by the child's manipulation of concrete objects to learn about their shape, size, or number of objects in a set. The next higher level of representation of reality, the iconic level, deals with images and is exemplified educationally by the use of pictures of sets of objects. The highest level is the symbolic level and involves words and numerals (e.g., use of the numeral "5" or the spoken or written word *five* to represent the number fiveness is symbolic). Thus, the use of mathematics workbooks in kindergarten and the early grades involves the iconic and symbolic levels and should *follow* object manipulation which is the enactive level. These may be thought of as levels of learning.

4. Gagne, R. M. "The Acquisition of Knowledge." *Psychological Review,* 62 (1962):355–65. Gagne's concept of "learning hierarchies" refers to analyzing a skill to be learned into its component parts and arranging them in an appropriate learning sequence.

5. ———. *The Conditions of Learning,* pp. 58–59. New York: Holt, Rinehart and Winston, 1965. Gagne has classified eight "types of learning" and described conditions necessary for their acquisition. Notice that the upper three levels of Gagne's hierarchy correspond with Brownell's concepts, principles or generalizations, and problem solving.

6. Horn, Alice. *The Uneven Distribution of the Effects of Specific Factors.* Southern California Education Monographs, No. 12. University of Southern California Press, 1941. (Later unpublished research studies, Evaluation section, Los Angeles City Schools.)

7. Piaget, Jean. *Child's Conception to Number.* New York: W. W. Norton and Co., 1965.

8. Piaget discusses two concepts of reversibility: "reversibility of inversion" exemplified by pouring the marbles from the cup to the pan and imagin-

ing the consequences of reversing this act, and "reversibility by reciprocity" which underlies the activity of comparing two rows of objects, one of which contains four objects, while the other row contains six, although both rows are of the same length. (Here the lack of density of the four-object row compensates for the increase in length to allow this row to be the same length as the six-object row.)

9. Jean Piaget has theorized that children's concepts of time and of duration depend on speed. ". . . one does not find that the young child has a concept of time which is radically independent of speed" (Piaget, 1966, p. 208).

Two different entities, succession of events and duration, are components of the notion of time. "Succession of events" refers to temporal order; "duration" is the interval between separate events. Piaget has discussed the ordinal notion of simultaneity which he illustrates in the following experiment:

> We put two dolls on the table in front of the child and make them leave from the same place, side by side, and then stop beside one another. At the moments when they start and stop we make an audible click as a signal. We then ask the children if the dolls started at the same time or not, and whether they stopped at the same time or not. If the two moving dolls have the same speed and if they leave from the same place and stop at the same place, the children have no difficulty in telling that the dolls started and stopped at the same time. If, however, the speeds are changed so that the two dolls have the same starting point and the same stopping time but one of them reaches a more distant point, the results are different. All the children agree that the dolls started at the same time, that the departures are simultaneous. . . . They do not agree that the instants of arrival were simultaneous, for the moving dolls were not stopped at the same point.
>
> . . . 'at the same time' is a phrase having no meaning for the young child. . . . 'At the same time' has meaning only in the situation where the two dolls stayed next to each other throughout the entire trip. For movements of different velocities, with different points of arrival in space, simultaneity does not yet have significance because *the coordination of the time of one movement with the time of another movement presupposes a real understanding of the structure of time.*
>
> At about six years of age, while the child admits simultaneity, he does not yet conceive of the equality of synchronized durations. (The dolls) the child agrees . . . have left at the same time and . . . have stopped at the same time. But if . . . asked whether one doll had moved for the same length of time as the other did . . . reply

is that one of them moved for a longer time because it has traveled further.

. . . to make a comparison of movements through the same distances but at different velocities one finds two distinct steps.

First, where the child replies 'that ones goes faster and (consequently) takes more time: and afterwards, the child says, 'that one is faster and (consequently) takes less time.' . . . *the first reply depends upon the result* (faster is equated with farther and consesequently with more time) and *the second upon* the process itself (faster means less time). The second case, thus, expresses some operations which bear on the transformation as such and not simply on the stationary result of configuration (Piaget, 1966, pp. 208–309.)*

Piaget also used cars in place of dolls (Piaget, 1955, p. 36). I used cars in my study (Reisman, 1968) believing them to be a less sex-bound stimulus than were dolls. The car tasks were as follows:

Task 1. Both cars start at same place, travel at same speed, for the same duration of time. They stop at same place.

$$X\text{-------------}\rightarrow X$$
$$X\text{------------}\rightarrow X$$

Task 2. Both cars start at same place, travel at different speeds, and for the same duration of time. They stop at different places.

$$X\text{------}\rightarrow X$$
$$X\text{--------}\rightarrow X$$

Task 3. Both cars start at same place, travel at same speeds, and for different durations of time. They stop at different places.

$$X\text{------}\rightarrow X$$
$$X\text{----------}\rightarrow X$$

Task 2 was the crucial activity so far as the system of time measurement is concerned because the measurement of time is dependent upon the understanding of the "coordination of operations of temporal succession and time duration. . . ."

---

* Reprinted from "Time Perception in Children" by Jean Piaget. In *The Voices of Time,* edited by J. T. Fraser (New York: George Braziller, 1966; London: Penguin Books, 1966), by permission of the publishers and author.

Prior to that time nothing is gained by the utilization of a watch . . . because the small child of four to six years does not understand that the speed of movement of hands on a watch is constant. For example, if the child observes a watch in order to estimate the time taken by an object to execute a rapid movement, the hand of the watch appears to him to move more slowly than if he tries to estimate the time taken by an object in slower motion . . . the child sees no reason why he should assume that the rate of displacement of the watch hand . . . is constant. He has not yet the intellectual tools to understand the problem of conservation of speed. . . . The development of systematic time concepts is . . . at no point independent of the understanding of concepts of speed (Piaget, 1955, p. 41).*

According to Piaget, success on Task 2 does not occur before the ages of seven or eight:

. . . . let us consider the situation in which two moving bodies start simultaneously from the same point: B moving more rapidly than A has covered more distance at the moment of simultaneous arrest. Here, children of approximately four to six years of age admit without difficulty the simultaneity of departure but not that of arrest. Yet, this is not due to any perceptual errors. The subject acknowledges easily that when B stops, A no longer moves, and vice versa. He refuses to say, however, that the objects came to rest at the same time, 'together.' The child thinks B stopped 'before' A because the former is 'ahead' of the latter in the spatial sense; or else he thinks that A stopped before B stopped 'first' in the sense that it is spatially closer. . . . in summary it can be said that, at the 'preoperative' level of development, the child's judgments of simultaneity or successiveness in time depend on the equality or inequality of the speed of objects moving along the same path (Piaget, 1955, pp. 36–37).

I found that although first grades could reproduce and identify time on a clockface (which are skills), most of the third graders did not have the concepts necessary for an *understanding* of time measurement. (Reisman, 1968).

10. Reisman, Fredricka K. "Children's Errors in Telling Time and a Recommended Teaching Sequence." *The Arithmetic Teacher.* 18, 3 (March 1971): pp. 152–55.

---

* Reprinted from "The Development of Time Concepts in the Child" by Jean Piaget. In *Psychopathology of Childhood,* edited by Paul Hoch and Joseph Lubin (New York: Grune and Stratton, 1955), by permission of the publisher and the author.

11. ———. "An Evaluative Study of Cognitive Acceleration in Mathematics in the Early School Years." Ph.D. dissertation, Syracuse University, 1968.

12. Slosson, Richard L., *The Slosson Intelligence Test for Children and Adults* (SIT). 146 Pine Street, East Aurora, N. Y.; Slosson Educational Publications is a short, easy to administer, individual IQ test. A broad population was used for establishing reliability and validity measures. The author states in his manual, "In summary, this Short Intelligence Test (SIT) yields sufficiently valid IQ's, for children four years of age into adulthood, as to furnish a useful screening instrument in the hands of responsible, professional persons. No significant sex differences were found for any of these age groups. For children under four years of age, the IQ's must always be considered as tentative."

13. Taba, Hilda, and Elkins, Deborah. *Teaching Strategies for the Culturally Disadvantaged,* p. 7. Chicago: Rand McNally and Company, 1966.

14. John W. Wilson who is presently Professor of Mathematics Education at the University of Maryland, College Park, found this procedure of identifying the wanted—given situation very helpful for the problem-solver. This conclusion was based on his doctoral research: "The Role of Structure in Verbal Problem-Solving in Arithmetic." Unpublished Ph.D. dissertation, Syracuse University, 1964.

15. My thanks to Richard Brice, Chapel Hill, University of North Carolina, for sharing many of these with me.

16. Dunn, L. M. *Peabody Picture Vocabulary Test.* Circle Pines, Minnesota: American Guidance Service, 1965.

17. Wechsler, D. *Wechsler Intelligence Scale for Children (Wisc).* New York: Psychological Corporation, 1967.

18. Terman, Lewis M. and Merrill, Maud A. *Stanford-Binet Intelligence Scale Manual for the Third Revision, Form L-M.* Boston: Houghton-Mifflin Company, 1962.

Suggested Readings

Braun, Charles. "Familiarity Breeds Understanding." *Arithmetic Teacher,* 16: (April 1969): 316–17 +.

Glennon, Vincent J. "Enrichment Mathematics For the Grades." In *27th Yearbook of the National Council of Teachers of Mathematics,* edited by Vincent J. Glennon. Washington, D.C.: National Council of Teachers of Mathematics, 1963.

Glennon, Vincent J.; Mueller, Francis J.; and Anderson, Richard M. *Essential Modern Mathematics: Book D,* Teacher's Edition. Boston: Ginn and Co., 1970.

Glennon, Vincent J., Mueller, Francis J., and Dutton, Wilbur H. *Essential Modern Mathematics: Book C,* Teacher's Edition. Boston: Ginn and Co., 1970.

Glennnon, Vincent J., Riedesel, Alan C.; and Suydam, Marilyn N. *Essential Modern Mathematics: Book B,* Teacher's Edition. Boston: Ginn and Co., 1970.

Glennon, Vincent J.; Weaver, Fred J.; and Armstrong, Jenny R. *Essential Modern Mathematics: Book A,* Teacher's Edition. Boston: Ginn and Co., 1970.

Krathwohl, David R.; Bloom, Benjamin S.; and Masia, Bertram B. *Taxonomy of Educational Objectives, Handbook 2: Affective Domain.* New York: David McKay Co., 1966.

Mager, R. F. *Preparing Instructional Objectives.* Palo Alto, California: Fearon Publishers, 1962.

Maslow, Abraham H. *Motivation and Personality.* New York: Harper and Row, 1954.

————. "Some Basic Propositions of a Growth and Self-Actualization Psychology." In *Perceiving, Behaving, Becoming, A New Focus for Education,* 1962 Yearbook, chairman, Arthur W. Combs, pp. 34–39. Washington, D.C.: Association for Supervision and Curriculum Development.

McGillivray, R. H. "Differences in Home Background Between High–Achieving and Low–Achieving Gifted Children: A study of 108 Pupils in the City of Toronto Public Schools." *Ontario Journal of Educational Research* 6(1964):99–106.

Mumpower, D. L., and Riggs, Sharon. "Overachievement in Word Accuracy as a Result of Parental Pressure." *The Reading Teacher,* vol. 28, no. 8 (May 1970).

Osgood, C.; Suci, G.; and Tannenbaum, P. *The Measurement of Meaning.* Urbana, Ill.: University of Illinois Press, 1967.

Piaget, Jean. "The Development of Time Concepts in the Child." In *Psychopathology of Childhood,* edited by Paul Hoch and Joseph Cuben, pp. 34–44.

183

New York: The Proceedings of the Forty–fourth Annual Meeting of the American Psychopathological Association, June 1955; New York: Grune and Stratton, 1955.

————. "Time Perception in Children." In *The Voices of Time,* edited by J. T. Fraser, pp. 202–16. New York: George Braziller, 1966.

Pierce, J. V. "Personality and Achievement among Able High School Boys." *Journal of Individual Psychology* 17 (1961): 101–102.

Popham, James W., and Baker, Eva L. *Establishing Instructional Goals.* Englewood Cliffs, New Jersey: Prentice-Hall, 1970.

Reisman, Fredricka K. "An Evaluative Study of Cognitive Acceleration in Mathematics in the Early School Years." Ph.D. dissertation, Syracuse University, 1968. (Available in microfilm or Xerographic copy from University Microfilms, Ann Arbor, Michigan, 302 pp.)

————. *Diagnostic Teaching of Elementary School Mathematics: Methods and Content.* Skokie, Illinois: Rand McNally, 1977.

Reisman, Fredricka K., and Kauffman, Samuel H. *Teaching Mathematics to Children with Special Educational Needs.* Columbus, Ohio: Charles E. Merrill Co. (in press).

Rogers, Carl R. "Significant Learning: In Therapy and in Education." *Educational Leadership* 16 (January 1959): 4.

————. "A Theory of Therapy, Personality, and Interpersonal Relationships." In *Psychology: A Study of Science.* Vol. 3, *Formulations of the Person and the Social Context,* edited by S. Koch, pp. 185–256. New York: McGraw-Hill, 1959.

Rouman, Jack. "School Childrens' Problems as Related to Parental Factors." *Journal of Educational Research* 50 (October 1956): 105.

Name Index

Subject Index